PRAISE FOR *GEARED FOR LIFE*

"The success of our Grave Digger team over the last 40+ years isn't the result of luck or skill. We fought with everything we had for years to keep the dream alive. We learned. We failed. We won. We lost. But we always seemed to find another gear we never knew we had to move forward. That's what *Geared for Life* will equip you to do. Bryce's perspective is dead on in this book."

—Dennis Anderson, Driver & Creator of the Grave Digger Monster Jam truck, Monster Jam Hall of Fame Inductee, and 4X World Finals Champion

"There is no secret formula to success in motorsports or in anything, really. It takes heart, patience, getting the right people around you, and maybe being a little stubborn when you're chasing your dream. This book, *Geared for Life*, will help you get that mindset and help you make those moves."

—John Force, 16-time NHRA champion, owner and CEO of John Force Racing

"Highly recommended! *Geared for Life* is a step-by-step guide for anyone wanting to live a meaningful life and ignite their passions again."

—Criss Angel, world-renowned magician and creator of television's biggest magic show in history, *Criss Angel: MINDFREAK*

"*Geared for Life* will inspire you to step out of your comfort zone, believe in yourself, and embark on a transformative journey. Throughout the book, Bryce Kenny reminds us that we are not alone in our struggles. He provides effective approaches on how to overcome fears and gain confidence to make a positive influence and live with purpose. This book equips you with the tools you need to shift into the right gear and unlock your greatness."

—Lisa Hake, Vice President of Marketing and Communications, Great Clips, Inc.

GEARED FOR LIFE

GEARED FOR LIFE

MAKING THE SHIFT INTO YOUR FULL POTENTIAL

BRYCE KENNY

DEXTERITY
NASHVILLE

DEXTERITY

Dexterity, LLC
604 Magnolia Lane
Nashville, TN 37211

Printed in the United States of America.
First edition: 2023
10 9 8 7 6 5 4 3 2 1

ISBN: 978-1-947297-78-4 (Hardcover)
ISBN: 978-1-947297-79-1 (E-book)
ISBN: 978-1-947297-90-6 (Audiobook)

Publisher's Cataloging-in-Publication data

Names: Kenny, Bryce, author.
Title: Geared for life: making the shift into your full potential / Bryce Kenny.
Description: Nashville, TN: Dexterity, 2023.
Identifiers: ISBN: 978-1-947297-78-4 (hardcover) | 978-1-947297-79-1 (ebook) | 978-1-947297-90-6 (audio)
Subjects: LCSH Success. | Leadership. | Self-actualization (Psychology) | Self-help. | Drag racing--Anecdotes. | Motorsports--Anecdotes. | Conduct of life. | BISAC SELF-HELP / Personal Growth / Success | BUSINESS & ECONOMICS / Leadership | SELF-HELP / Motivational & Inspirational
Classification: LCC BF637.S4 .K46 2023 | DDC 158.1--dc23

Cover design by Faceout Studio
Interior design by PerfecType, Nashville

DEDICATION

For McKenzie, who is the only proof I've ever needed that God must have a plan for my life.

CONTENTS

WARM UP

"Life is hard. It's even harder when you're stupid."
—John Wayne

I was traveling late one night from my North Carolina home to my family's race shop in Kentucky. I had made this six-hour trip at least ten times that year in my 2001 Mustang with the five-speed manual transmission, but this trip was different. I was trying out a shorter route through the mountains of Virginia in the middle of the night. How stupid.

Around 1:00 a.m., it started to rain. Then fog set in. My phone lost all cell service, causing my GPS to quit working, so I was completely lost. I was OK until I looked down at my dashboard and saw that I had less than a quarter of a tank of gas. "No problem," I thought. "I'll just stop at the next gas station to get some fuel and make sure I'm headed in the right direction."

Thirty minutes went by without a gas station in sight or even a passing car on the winding road. I had managed to pick a route that threw me a mountainous curve every mile or so, each one requiring me to slow to about 25–35 mph. Panic finally set in when my fuel light came on and I still had no cell service. My left knuckles had turned white from my tight grip on the steering wheel, plus my right elbow was starting to ache from my constant shifting of the manual transmission into higher gears on the straightaways and then back down to first or second gear at the mouth of every curve. At times like this, I would normally be accompanied by a Garth Brooks tune blasting through my radio, but I had turned that off about an hour and a half earlier when the rain and fog first arrived.

The more disoriented I became, the slower I drove. Any slower and I would be creeping. Each mile slowly chipped away at my optimism that I would avoid being stranded overnight with near-freezing temps outside. At that point, I was no longer concerned about making it to my destination. I was hyper-focused on every shift of the transmission, every curve in the road, and vigilantly scanning the tree line for any sort of gas station sign that might be hiding.

After another ninety minutes of dread-filled concentration, I finally saw a gas station as I came around a curve. I threw the transmission into neutral, coasted until I rolled into the parking lot, and crawled to a stop at the pump. I sat in my car for five minutes to collect myself, lower my heart rate, and find the energy and motivation to keep the road trip going. As soon as I got out of the car, my phone's cell service magically came back on and updated my route. I eventually reached my destination around 4:00 a.m. I've never again flirted with taking that same treacherous route!

Life can be the same way. Just like those unexpected experiences when you're disoriented while driving on a twisting mountainous road on a foggy night, your life situations can suddenly cause you to decelerate, turn the music down, and sharpen your focus on the task at hand. If, though, you don't know what gears you have available to shift into in life, how can you expect to get through the tough situations? What if I'd had only first gear available in my car for that anxiety-ridden road trip, resulting in terrible fuel mileage and preventing me from gaining speed on the straightaway parts of my journey? What if I only had fifth gear? Surely I wouldn't have been able to adapt to the slow, mountainous curves. What if I had decided just to sit on the side of the road all night in neutral until a good Samaritan stopped to help?

I needed all five gears to get through that night.

Once we understand *what* gears are available to us in life and *when* to shift into them, we avoid becoming stuck. Instead, we keep momentum. The secret to getting to the finish line is *momentum*, not some hidden formula for success reserved for people of a certain background, creed, or color. If you're overly focused on the finish line where you hope your dreams await you, but don't know how or when to shift along the way, you might quickly become frustrated, defeated, and stuck.

The core of this book is a collection of my seven gears—my personal foundational truths—that have propelled me around and over obstacles thrown in my path that threatened to prevent me from reaching my finish line.

Life is too short to suck at living it well. To be fair, though, life can be really difficult. The John Wayne quote at the beginning of this introduction sums up how and why I have made my life harder than it had to be. My stupidity at times hasn't been from a lack of intelligence but from an abundance of unused opportunities. For many years I didn't realize the gears were at my disposal to use to my advantage. Sometimes I wasn't willing to move forward until I was positive I would win my race, so I just sat at the starting line idling, unwilling to shift and push forward. I hadn't seen my finish line—my desired destination—in a long time. In hindsight, that might explain why life felt monotonous. All day long I would suffer silently, daydreaming about the moment my head would hit the pillow that night, only to then lie in bed staring at the ceiling asking, "Is this really all there is to life?" Something had to shift.

I was fortunate to answer that question for myself at a young age, but it came at a cost I will share with you throughout this book. I will share my personal stories about how I identified what my gears are and how I've learned to recognize the right time to shift into each one. I've had moments where I decided how to live my life based on what I believed my *purpose* was, not on how it would affect my bank account. I've had to learn what it looks like to become built for *others* instead of looking out only for my own ambitions. I've learned to prioritize making *memories* with the people in my life ahead of stroking my own ego—one of my seven gears. That wasn't easy for a young guy craving to make a name for himself in the racing world.

The world never taught me to do what was *right* regardless of the consequences; I had to learn it on my own, while getting knocked down a few pegs along the way. The rest of the gears I share here will open your mind to identifying your own. You're welcome to borrow mine, but I have a sneaky suspicion that as you work your way through this book, you'll begin to discover your own gears and foundational beliefs that you've kept bottled up for far too long.

Whether you're in high school scuffling to figure out your direction after graduation, a young professional striving to find the passion to become the best employee in your company, a single mom just trying to make it through the day, a successful business owner who feels like you've plateaued, or someone following any one of hundreds of other paths of life out there, you need to be willing to look under your metaphorical hood and discover the gears you have available to get unstuck and get into gear.

I've lived parts of my life stuck in neutral, making a lot of noise without going anywhere. At the other end of the track, I've stubbornly raced toward my dreams as fast as humanly possible, pouring twenty hours a day into chasing my ambitions but really going nowhere while simply measuring activity and expecting results. The race *you* run toward your goal(s) cannot be fueled by a shallow resolve to outwork everyone else. You have to learn how to find the right gear at the right time to accelerate to speeds you never imagined were possible. The only way to do that is to have a clear understanding of which gears you have at your fingertips.

The best race car drivers don't always have the fastest car, but they know how to utilize the gears most effectively. Maybe you have more fuel in your tank than you realize. Maybe all you need to do is find another gear you never knew you had. Maybe all you need to do is make your next shift. I hope this book serves to open your mind, restore your hope, and put you back in the driver's seat with the pedal down and headed toward living the life you've always wanted. If so, the many hours I have put into this project will have been well worth it.

Throw on your helmet, strap in tight, feel that throttle pedal underneath your foot, and let's start that engine. It's time to get *Geared for Life*!

1

STALLED

Get Out of Neutral

In 2013, I was fired from my first "big" job and escorted out of the building. I was not laid off for budgetary reasons; I was fired. Terminated. I had always thought this sort of thing was reserved for bad employees and people—the "other guys"—who created problems for an organization, not me. I was furious and embarrassed with one dreadful thought consuming me: "How did my life get to this point?"

When I awoke that day, I figured it would be a normal Monday. I ate a normal breakfast. I had a normal conversation with my new wife, McKenzie. I barely hit any red lights on the way to my office at the North Carolina Youth Soccer Association. The Monday morning staff meeting was painfully boring. Afterward, I went to grab my second cup of coffee so I could get settled into work at my desk. About forty-five minutes later, our executive director (let's call her Robin) asked to see me in her office. She looked like she was about to conduct a funeral. I was clueless that it was my corporate coffin she was nailing shut.

As I walked into Robin's office, our organization's president (let's call him Kevin) stood there waiting for us. He quickly commanded me to "sit down" in the type of judgmental tone reserved for a courtroom sentencing.

"Bryce, it has come to our attention that you are not committed to the direction we're taking this organization," Kevin said. "We've decided to terminate your employment, effective immediately."

"Excuse me? Why am I being *fired*?" I asked.

"Like I said, we do not feel that you have bought into this new direction we're going in," he answered.

I was beyond confused. I won't go into detail explaining all the work I *had been doing* to help lead the organization in its new direction; suffice it to say, there had to be another reason.

"I am not leaving here until you explain to me why I'm being fired! How am I supposed to go home and explain this to my wife?"

"You will leave this office, or we will call the police!" Kevin said.

Great. Not only was I embarrassed and angry, now I was being threatened. How could this get so bad, so quickly? I looked over at Robin and threw up my hands as if to say, "Don't you have anything to add?" She sat there quietly, looking down at her desk without muttering a word. I knew if I didn't leave, the situation was going to get worse. So I packed up my personal stuff from my desk and stormed out with my two-week severance check.

I got home about two hours before McKenzie did, and all I could do was sit on the couch and rehearse what I would say to her. I wanted to avoid saying anything that might make her panic or think we'd be homeless within a month. We had no savings, and losing half of our household income when we each made about $28,000 a year before taxes wasn't what she could have imagined for our first year of marriage. Finally, she got home, walked in the door, and surprised to see me, said, "Well, you're home early!"

"I've got good news and bad news," I said. "The bad news is that I got fired today. Like, terminated. Let go. The good news is that I have an interview set up for Wednesday with an executive search firm that called me last week."

Her look of panic remains scarred in my memory. Any security she had felt in our home before that moment vanished. She stood there with her mouth open as tears filled her eyes. All she could say was, "What are we going to do?" I didn't have a decent answer to give her, but I reassured her that we'd figure it out.

Here's the back story on the executive search firm. The Friday before I got fired, the CEO had called me with some questions following a training seminar I had given a few weeks earlier regarding coaching rec soccer. He'd been volunteered by his wife to coach his daughter's rec team and had attended the seminar to pick up some extra tips. He was impressed with the way I handled the seminar and was curious if I was open to hearing about an opportunity to work with his firm. I responded, "Absolutely, I am!" He had then called me at my desk one business day before (separated by the weekend) I got fired asking me to come interview with his firm. Talk about a thin thread! After my second interview, they called me that evening with a job offer to start the following Monday. Between the two-week severance from the soccer organization and my almost-immediate start in my new job, I never missed a single paycheck.

That was the day I stopped believing in coincidences.

When life stalls out, we're left with moments of panic and uncertainty. We freeze. Whether it's a dreaded medical diagnosis, the death of a family member, the loss of a vital source of income that threatens survival, or some other event that makes you feel like your life has smacked head-on into a telephone pole, what you believe at your core will determine when you get back into motion. Everyone stalls out at some point in their life. But if you know and trust what you believe, those beliefs can serve as gears you're able to shift to get back into motion. Instead of waiting for some secret formula to fall out of the sky showing you how to overcome a bad situation, focus on finding the right gear to shift yourself into moving toward a solution.

After I was fired, I had a decision to make. I could wallow in self-pity and become stuck in neutral for the foreseeable future, or I could look at what was in my heart to see if there was something in there that would get my life back into gear. I had tried to build a life of safety and comfort with my soccer organization job, only to have it swiped away, leaving me holding my bag on the street corner outside of my office with a severance check. It was then that I grasped how I had allowed my deepest longings in life to become dormant.

My dreams of racing and having a platform seemed far too distant without any glaring opportunities in front of me.

For me, a platform meant being in a position of influence in hopes of making a lasting impact on other people in a meaningful way. Instead, I was living in a world that put a premium on happiness above all else and found myself constantly asking, "Is this really all there is to life?" Idling in neutral had become natural for me. I desperately needed to make a shift. But to make the right adjustment, I had to understand what mode I was in.

Most newer cars on the road today give drivers the option to change driving mode to "Eco," "Off-road," or "Sport." Each mode adjusts the setup of the car to adapt to the driver's situation. Similarly, we're operating our lives in one of the following modes right now:

- **"Stalled"**

  Stuck. No movement. You're in the garage up on jack stands. Engine is blown up. Can't figure out how to get moving again. Confused. Frustrated. Opportunities feel rare. And if opportunity did show up, you'd only see it as risk instead of potential. "Is this really all there is to life?"

- **"In Gear"**

  You're on the track. You're moving. You might not know if you're going to be fast, but you're taking action. You find opportunities. 1+1=2 and your efforts are turning into some results. "How long will you have to keep this effort up?"

- **"Racing"**

  You're on the track and accelerating. You've got momentum. Results feel easy to attain. You're excited to wake up in the morning and find out what's in store. One good thing turns into another. Opportunities seem to find you. 1+1=11. You have the freedom to ask yourself, "What would I do today if I knew I couldn't fail?"

I had been stuck in "stalled" mode for a few years until the soccer organization fired me. This is the most difficult mode to get out of because we don't always know when we're in it. This mode has the least amount of self-awareness attached to it, so people stay in it for a long time without realizing it. I knew, though, that I couldn't create or turn on momentum like a light switch. I had to get back in gear before I could move into racing mode where momentum thrived.

Life isn't so much about consistently getting everything right as it is about being willing to change that blown tire on the side of the highway when life throws you screws (or nails). Life is about taking action with the small stuff along the way, and then leveraging momentum as far as you can for as long as you can. Being trained to see what real momentum looks like gives you the confidence needed to take more risks, have more faith that it'll all work out, and be creative enough to use momentum to produce results in your daily life.

If you've been parked on the side of the road waiting for answers, maybe it's time we get you back into racing mode! The best news in all this: you have more control over which mode you operate in than you realize. So let's get you back on the racetrack and in racing mode, shifting through one gear at a time to reach the record-breaking speeds you're capable of.

SHIFTING OUT OF "STALLED" MODE

I now understand why getting fired was a pivotal moment for me and that it was meant to happen. It *needed* to happen. If I'd still had my job with the soccer organization when I interviewed and got the job offer at the executive search firm, I probably would not have taken it. The soccer organization gave me a lot of flexibility with my time, and I didn't know a thing about executive recruiting. I believe, however, there was a sovereign entity that knew I needed a nudge (or in my case, a shove) in the right direction. Being axed took the decision out of my hands.

Sometimes those life moments that feel like a crash are just course corrections for the better, putting you on the next racecourse you are meant to run. Holding on to such a perspective allows you to be patient enough to leverage each failure into something greater than yourself. It helps you develop an appetite for risk and a "can't lose" mentality that allows momentum to operate in your life.

Once I became OK with the fact that I had lessons I needed to learn and shifts I needed to make to become the best version of myself, I welcomed the obstacles. When I realized I was built to jump over the obstacles that came in my path, I no longer wanted to idle in neutral. Making the shifts became desirable. Getting yourself back in gear can be as simple as being willing to accept the vulnerable position that comes with a life in motion.

Even though the road I took wasn't easy, I shifted into a successful career with the executive search firm. Talking to C-suite executives all day developed a skillset in me that I utilize everyday in my professional motorsports career when I interact with brands, partners, and fans. There isn't a boardroom that would make me nervous to stand in or a stage I'd be unwilling to speak on. That's a direct result of my stint as an executive recruiter. But how did I make the shift from executive recruiting to Monster Jam? Don't worry. I'll get to that in a future chapter. It's a fun story!

GETTING BACK "IN GEAR"

As a professional driver, the safest place for me is when I'm idling. The most comfortable place for me is at a standstill. But a Monster Jam truck wasn't built for neutral gear. It was built to engage 1,500 horsepower at 7,000 rpm to jump 30 feet in the air and do backflips! You aren't built for a life in neutral either. You're built for a life in motion and to push through the hard stuff to become the best possible version of yourself.

As I sat in my house during my two-week transition between being fired from the soccer organization and starting at the executive search firm, I realized that at some point in the previous year I had lost my focus on what I was built for. The best opportunities don't come from safety or comfortable situations. My best opportunities were results of momentum that arose from my foundational beliefs that drove my actions. But I had sacrificed all momentum for the hope of a robust retirement plan. I had succumbed to analyzing the best benefits packages instead of seeking my purpose. I had bought into the lie from society that our goal should be to eventually arrive safely at a cemetery.

Once I realized the mistake I had made, I immediately began a quest to regain momentum and get back on track. Even before that, though, I spent time contemplating my life and where I had been. Through that reflection I eventually came to understand what I believe, why I believe it, and how those beliefs had shaped my decision-making along the way. Being "in gear" simply means taking action toward the things you want most in life.

You shape your environment through your actions. So changing your life requires you to change your actions, and that requires defining what you believe. That's the key to staying in gear. But staying in gear can't be the end goal. You want to be in "racing" mode, where you are able to realize your full potential!

FINDING YOUR RACING MODE

The question I get asked the most as a professional Monster Jam driver is, "Does it hurt when you land?" The honest answer is, "It depends." Driving a Monster Jam truck is all about momentum. Jumping a 12,000-pound truck thirty feet in the air isn't going to produce a comfortable landing. But the best way to explain why landing with momentum doesn't hurt is what I will call the "bucket principle." Imagine you're standing on a five-gallon bucket turned upside down. If you step off the bucket, you'll get jarred on the landing. But imagine you start walking fast toward the bucket from about fifteen feet away, step on it without breaking your stride, and then step off it to continue your movement. The landing isn't going to be as rough. That's how it feels driving a Monster Jam truck. It is all about *momentum*.

From my vantage point, life is the same way. The more momentum you have, the easier it is to get over the bumps. You're less phased by the issues in your path. Many people are stuck standing on top of their metaphorical five-gallon bucket, afraid to step off for fear of the pain. They've lost momentum and aren't sure how to regain it. It's time to change that.

Merriam-Webster defines *momentum* as "strength or force gained by motion or by a series of events." Momentum comes in waves and *never* lasts forever. Shifting into the right gear at the right time is what produces and encourages momentum. Like a 4x4 truck on a back road, sometimes you need to shift up into fifth gear on a flat spot of the road in order to gain speed. Other times, you come up on a big hill with rocks and need to shift back down into first gear.

Life is the same way; it requires us to shift into the right gear at the right time. That's the secret to momentum. The difference between a successful person and an unsuccessful person isn't skill sets or luck. A successful person has simply capitalized on moments of momentum. When you know what the different gears are, you gain strength or force by motion or by a series of events in order to get momentum working on your behalf.

MAKING THE NEXT SHIFT

I get to live this crazy life as a professional Monster Jam driver, but I admit that life has been far from smooth to get me to this point. My foundational beliefs and having the courage to keep moving have shifted me onto this massive platform on a global stage, with a wife and three kids by my side every step of the way.

The seven "gears" described in the following chapters have been shift points for me. Life is messy and disorienting, but these gears have kept momentum on my side to help me get through any situation life throws at me. They've been foundational beliefs for me, absolute truths that I can defend to anyone. I also believe these shift points will help you get unstuck and move past your own self-doubts, fears, and obstacles that have kept you from living the life you've always wanted. They will allow you to live in your strengths and utilize them in ways you hadn't previously considered. You'll finally have a clear picture of *who* you want to become, instead of just focusing on *what* you wish you were accomplishing. Don't give up on unlocking the best version of yourself. Are you ready to find that next gear?

TUNE-UP

1. Where do you currently find yourself in life: "stalled," "in gear," or "racing mode"?
2. If you're stalled, how did you end up in this predicament?
3. What life event have you allowed to be an excuse to keep you in your current mode? If you had to find a positive result from this difficult life event you endured, what would it be?

2

WINDSHIELD

Shifting Focus

One of my favorite things to do is give people a behind-the-scenes look inside my Great Clips Mohawk Warrior truck. My invitation is always met with two immediate reactions. The first: "Wow! You sit really high up in this thing!" The second: "I can't believe you can see where you're driving!" Everyone is always surprised to learn how I steer the front tires with a normal steering wheel using my left hand, but I control the back tires independently from the front with a small toggle that fits between my right thumb and forefinger. They also offer a you've-got-to-be-kidding-me look when I show them the ratchets I use to tighten the two seat belts strapped across my hips—making them so tight that breathing becomes a chore.

The driving mechanisms aren't the elements that seem odd to me. The one thing that still blows my mind is how I see out of the truck when I jump thirty feet in the air. Hitting a nine-foot-tall jump throws me like an arrow into the sky where only the upper level of the football stadium I'm competing in is visible through the windshield. When I show someone the clear plastic-like panels beside my feet that allow me to look down past the monstrous tires, they finally get a mental image of being so high in the air that a driver has to figure out how to pick a landing spot. That's when they usually say, "There's no way I could drive this thing!"

A good Monster Jam driver knows how to position the truck in the air to get a clear picture of where they're going to land. The four huge tires (they weigh eight hundred pounds each) become tools of physics that we use to control the pitch of the truck through centrifugal force, something learned from how dirt bikes work. To get the truck to level off in midair, I tap the brake to slow the rotation of the tires. To raise the angle of the truck (pitch), I give the truck some throttle to increase the tire speed, and centrifugal force does its thing. My ninth-grade physics teacher, Mr. Losey, would be so impressed!

THE BEST VERSION

Life is like adjusting the pitch of a monster truck to improve your vantage point. Before we start to shift gears, we have to ensure we have the best view of the track in front of us. Not having this clear picture of the track could lead to disaster when we start accelerating. When we can't see through the windshield to see where we're going in life, what must we adjust to change the view?

Anytime I consider shifting my focus, I think back to one of my favorite moments from a road trip with my grandfather when I was growing up. I was extremely close to him. Grandpa was a mentor, a friend, and a comedian most of the time. He was a true racer at heart who started out tuning Oldsmobiles in the 1960s then advanced to drag racing on abandoned airstrips.

A nationally recognized chiropractor during the week, Grandpa viewed drag racing as his weekend escape. He moved up the different classes in the sport through the years, bought and operated a drag strip in Clay City, Kentucky, in the nineties, and eventually owned and drove a Top Fuel dragster at the professional level in 2001. Top Fuel dragsters are the long, skinny cars you might have seen on TV that reach 300 mph in under four seconds before parachutes deploy after the finish line to slow them down. Dragsters produce more than 10,000 horsepower and send eight-foot-high flames out the exhaust as they accelerate to a speed three times as fast as a Major League Baseball pitcher's fastball.

I was thirteen years old when Grandpa bought a Top Fuel dragster, and I spent all my teenage years traveling with his team to races across North America. One trip was a forty-hour journey from Kentucky to Alberta, Canada. While crossing Indiana, we saw farms as far as the eye could see. I rode shotgun with my grandfather as he hauled a double-decker race trailer. These frequent road trips during my teen years were filled with laughs, conversations about life, and a good kind of silence.

We were passing a field when Grandpa noticed a worker in the distance.

"Bryce, look at that guy out there," he said. "He's barely doing anything. He looks lifeless. If you want to get ahead in life, you've got to work hard and look the part. When you show up to work, dress like you want to be there. Be ready for action. Don't let your unrealized dreams and uncultivated passions go to the grave with you like that guy seems to be doing."

I didn't want to break the news to him. I sat there quietly taking in what he said, but I'm one of those people who can't hide my facial expressions when I have something I want to say. He seemed surprised I wasn't reacting to his sage wisdom the way I usually did.

"What?" he asked.

I said, "Grandpa, *that* was a scarecrow."

A brief pause turned into so much laughter that tears filled our eyes. His poor eyesight wouldn't have been as big of a concern if he wasn't going to be the one driving our 300-mph race car the following day.

I've referenced his words from that moment many times in my life. The truth is, I've seen myself as the scarecrow—lifeless and feeling unequipped—more times than I care to admit. I've spent days standing in a metaphorical field serving very little purpose and wondering where I went wrong. I'd ask myself, "Is it me? Do I have what it takes to accomplish my goals or be anything more than this? Maybe this is all there is." While I wasn't scaring actual birds away from crops, I felt like I was scaring off life's dots from connecting to one another. If I was going to find a gear in life that I never knew I had, I couldn't see myself as a scarecrow stuck in the ground. I had to shift into seeing myself as the best version instead of the worst.

BARN FINDS

I love old hot rods. I own a 1970 Mustang Mach 1 that has been in my family since 1983. That was the year my grandfather and my uncle Dan bought it off the side of a Kentucky road. I bought it from Dan in 2003 for just $4,500 and restored it so I could drive it as my first car in high school. (Yes, I did burnouts in my high school's parking lot after the big game on Friday nights.) I hope it'll be an heirloom for my kids if they choose to own it one day. These old cars are becoming as rare as a Bigfoot sighting. Meanwhile I feel a duty to keep it on the road, which is what I have to remind myself each time I fork out more money for parts. I look at it this way: I'm preserving history.

Car guys always imagine driving down a back road and noticing a barn with a covered car inside, its headlight peeking out. The guy knocks on the door of the house to ask the owners about the car. Low and behold, it's a 1969 Camaro with a 396-cubic inch motor. The body needs some love and attention to restore it to its former glory, and the interior needs to be reupholstered. The owner decides to sell it, and the guy has found a hidden treasure.

These barn finds are rare, but that doesn't keep any of us from imagining the moment. Isn't it funny how we can see a car like this—for what it *could be* instead of its current state in that barn? On the other hand, why is it so difficult for us to see ourselves as our best version? Maybe you're a '69 Camaro that's been under a tarp for far too long. After a fresh paint job and finding the right gears, your value is far greater than what you might see in yourself right now. I choose to see you with "barn find" eyes. The question is, can you start to see yourself that way?

When you start seeing your best version of yourself, you begin noticing opportunities to utilize the good things about yourself instead of trying to fix all the imperfections you see reflected in the mirror. There is a time to work on your weaknesses, but it is your potential that enables you to open your mind to the possibilities of who you can ultimately become. When you visualize your best version of yourself, you begin to clearly see the impact you're capable of making. Then you almost subconsciously look for ways to make that impact happen through your strengths instead of wasting your life trying to fix your weaknesses.

IMPOSTOR SYNDROME

Back in 2019, I was feeling insanely inadequate in my career. I was struggling both on and off the track as a Monster Jam driver and brand ambassador. I wasn't winning on the track, and I wasn't increasing the team's value in our partnership with Great Clips. I was tired of all the demands that accompanied my professional life: the heavy travel, the content creation necessary to grow my social media, and the looming contract negotiations that needed to take place if I wanted to continue down this path. I was just going through the motions. I was good at everything but not great at anything.

I remember sitting down one day and thinking, "*Who* am I really hoping to become as a person through this chapter of life?" I was so focused on *what* I was doing both on and off the track that I only had one way to measure myself: failures were bad, and successes were good. When I started to focus on *who* I wanted to become, both the failures and successes built the end result I wanted to see in myself. This shift in perspective helped me gain more momentum in my career than anything else over the previous ten years. It has kept me tightly secured like the ratcheted seat belts I described earlier. I had to stop obsessing over what I wanted to do differently and start envisioning *who* I wanted to become. Wanting to be a good father to my kids is *identity*, not effort. But the desire to be a good father drives my effort to go outside and play with remote-controlled cars with my son. If I skipped the desire part and went straight to a checklist mentality, I might go outside to play with my son for a while, but I wouldn't be doing it with heart or kindness. When we lead with identity, the right action becomes automatic.

Impostor syndrome is usually described as chronic self-doubt that prevents a person from seeing his or her external success or competence. In plain language, you don't feel like you have what it takes to accomplish the task in front of you. You feel like a house of cards that will topple with the slightest breeze. Sometimes impostor syndrome sneaks up on you the moment you decide you want to find your next gear: "If I've gotten myself stuck in neutral, who am I to think I can shift out of it?" That's a dangerous cycle to get into. So, how do we break it?

When I shifted my focus to *who* I wanted to become, I landed on three main goals:

- Become someone who has more faith
- Become someone who is more creative
- Become someone who takes more risks

Let's take a look at each of these.

HAVE MORE FAITH

Motorsports is one of the most fragile industries in America. I'm talking in financial terms. When I failed in my professional drag racing pursuit, I did so because I didn't get enough sponsorship support. The racing industry is extremely cutthroat, with many teams attempting (and oftentimes succeeding) to steal sponsors from others. It's survival of the fittest. The moment you land a sponsor, you immediately start working on the next year to secure that sponsor for an additional season or back-load that sponsorship slot with an alternative.

When Great Clips partnered with Monster Jam in 2017 and ultimately asked me to be the driver of their truck, I entered the relationship with this "survival of the fittest" mindset. This unique industry dynamic drives my desire to work as hard as possible in hopes of becoming the best brand ambassador Great Clips has ever had. Landing a sponsor is hard enough; but keeping a sponsor requires constant value creation and teamwork. I envision a metaphorical hourglass being flipped over each time a new contract is signed. With this mindset, how can I feel secure enough to give the sponsorship my best effort and attention? One word: faith.

Thankfully, Great Clips and Monster Jam have such a harmonious relationship that our team has been able to build one of the most engaging partnerships ever seen in motorsports. I work relentlessly on our Great Clips partnership without regard to immediate gratification. I do this because I have faith that our relationship will continue to grow. Along those lines, I also had faith five years ago when presented with my first opportunity to speak publicly for five minutes at the Great Clips 2018 national convention. As a result of the success of that first opportunity, Great Clips and Monster Jam increased our stage time at the last two conventions with an hour-long slot for the Monster Jam Morning Show, which they invented just for us.

Faith pushed me to spend a hundred hours preparing for the original five-minute talk. Faith also pushed me to spend another hundred hours preparing for the Monster Jam Morning Show. I'm grateful that I get to work with an amazing team, one in which everyone has a hand around the metaphorical hourglass with the united goal of continually flipping it over for years to come.

But what is *faith*, exactly?

Some people would describe me as "a person of faith." That's a fair assessment: I do have a personal relationship with Jesus. God has steered every step of my life and connected dots I never could have connected on my own. However, the meaning of the word *faith* has been narrowed in our society to reference a person's religious leanings. Faith isn't only a religious thing, though. Having faith means to believe in something *and* to act on that belief whether you see the results yet or not. Faith is taking steps believing what you want will come to pass.

I believe faith is something every person exercises every day. For example, you used faith for your most recent family road trip. Let's use the Grand Canyon as a destination example. You believed the Grand Canyon existed, so you planned a trip itinerary. Maybe you rented an RV. You opened the app on your phone for directions and discovered you had a fifteen-hour drive ahead of you. You can believe the Grand Canyon is there and that the GPS on your phone will guide you each step of the way to get you to your destination. But you still must actually get into the car (or that sweet RV you rented), start it up, shift into drive, and take the route you planned. Belief without action is not faith. Believing while taking action to support your belief is *faith*.

Some people believe their lives can change, but they're sitting in the driveway wondering why they can't see their destination through the windshield. Believing in something isn't enough to create change. Acting on a belief is what brings the change you want in your life. If you're struggling to pay rent, believing money will magically appear isn't faith. When you believe you will find a solution to pay next month's rent, true faith will push you to take action toward making it happen. You might have to get creative, but sitting at home idling while believing the problem will somehow resolve itself won't work. So what role does creativity play in getting results?

BE MORE CREATIVE

I have a love-hate relationship with social media. Using it is an easy way to be a mouthpiece and get a message out to a lot of people, but I'm convinced it chips away at our mental health to see everyone's highlights instead of the day-to-day grind. According to social media, everyone has their life figured out. That's why I sometimes hesitate to post as much as I should to maximize engagement with fans and supporters.

A few years ago, I committed to growing my social media presence. I had heard a prominent marketing guru encourage people to make content they wanted to make instead of making the content they thought they were supposed to make. That got my engine revving. I stopped caring if people engaged with what I created and tried to find a way to have fun creating content. It took all the pressure off my shoulders to get data-driven results, and my mind started building the type of ideas I enjoyed creating. Bolstering my social media presence went from feeling like a chore to becoming a megaphone for me to engage with an audience.

Let me stop here briefly to tell you that I'm not saying or suggesting you need to go out and start growing *your* social media footprint or making motivational videos like I did. I only mention it as an example of something creative I did to help advance my career as a public figure, knowing this endeavor was a good fit for me. Now ask yourself—and think it through for however long it takes—to find a path of creativity that works for you and holds your interest long enough to sink your heart and soul into it. It's there inside of you. Once you find that morsel of creativity, go for it. If you can see it—that is, you can envision it—the road ahead of you should be clear sailing.

OK, back to ramping up my social media presence. My first several posts didn't get much traction, but I wasn't focused on the engagement. I was focused on the process. I kept trying different approaches. One Saturday morning, I was sitting in my hotel room before heading to the stadium for our Monster Jam event in Houston and an idea came to me as I reviewed some videos saved on my phone. I thought, "What if I voiced-over a slow-motion video of one of my monster truck crashes and described what was going through my mind as I tried to drive the truck back onto its four tires?" So I tried it. Right now, that video has nearly five million views on one platform alone.

Five million! Are you kidding me? I'm not a natural right-brain, artistic person; I'm a left-brain, calculated thinker. I couldn't believe this idea actually worked! Was it just a fluke? It turns out I had discovered a niche. I've found that any video I post of me driving my monster truck that includes my voice-over explaining what's happening performs extremely well, producing hundreds of thousands of views. If I post a video of a crash or a backflip set to music, it doesn't perform as well. Add my voice-over to it, and it performs. The style and delivery of my voice were somehow connecting with that specific social media audience. I just had to be patient enough to allow some of my failed posts to stir my creative juices toward finding my next niche with content I wanted to create.

I believe being creative digs far deeper than artistic marketing approaches. For most of us, creative power becomes most valuable when we're forced to find solutions to our life's problems. Few life situations come with a manual that has a "troubleshooting" section in the back describing a solution. Whether you have a social media following or have never even created an online account, you should approach your life with the belief that good things can happen, that your actions can turn your beliefs into real results, and that you can commit to thinking outside the box to find your own niche in the process. Once you operate in faith and commit to creatively finding your niche, you're prepared to start taking more risks. I believe a person's appetite for risk determines his or her time frame for growth. But let's unpack that a bit, shall we?

TAKE MORE RISKS

We all know people who *always* talk about opportunities and their newest ideas but never give any of them the green light. It's like hearing the punchline of the same joke for the fifth time; it made you laugh the first time, but now it's annoying. Aspire to be someone capable of making a decision. Becoming someone who is comfortable with *risk* is part of that equation.

I have a friend who is a full-time real estate professional. I knew Matt long before he bought his first property. I once interviewed him on our *Live Like Warriors* podcast in an episode titled "Risky Business," where we talked about how we knew each other before either of us achieved a successful career. If our respective career paths were races, the first few laps did not go well for either of us.

It always seems that when the green light drops on a new venture, we all learn the most difficult lessons at the beginning. Matt told some hilarious stories about his first few house flips and the moments that made him question if he was built to be a real estate investor. He shared that if it weren't for the father of one of his friends who took pity on his bad luck during those first few investments, he wouldn't have found a way to keep moving forward. Flipping houses required Matt to stretch his mind to figure out how to take the right risks. Just because he could get a house at a cheap price didn't mean it was the right investment.

My first year of driving a Monster Jam truck was only a hobby. It was difficult for me to see a career in Monster Jam since I had a lucrative corporate career at the time. Just because I had an offer to go full-time into Monster Jam didn't mean it was the right choice. Just because there is risk doesn't make a decision right. What does make it right is understanding if the risk fits with the broader vision of who you're wanting to become through it all.

I knew I wanted to have a career in motorsports, so the offer to go full-time into Monster Jam aligned with that goal. Matt knew he wanted to be a full-time real estate professional instead of giving soccer lessons at preschools (his real job when he started real estate). Pushing through the hard stuff at the beginning made sense for him. By the way, Matt now has a $5.5 million real estate portfolio and golfs three times a week. His risk of learning a new industry and the financial risk of investing in real estate is clearly paying off. He stayed committed long enough to see the fruits of his labor.

Many people give up the race on those first few laps, when that's the time they're finally getting equipped with the knowledge of how to go on and win their race. Your ability to stomach risk determines how long it will take you to find the reward. I don't mean to suggest that you should throw caution to the wind. Sometimes the only way to learn which risks are worth taking is to lose. But as we will discuss in the next chapter, learning how to fail forward and fail faster are lessons every successful person has learned at some point in their journey.

My advice is to find the type of risks that build toward *who* you want to become, not *what* you want to possess. Meaning, don't go get your master's degree just for the piece of paper. Get your master's degree so you can start making the impact at your company that you've always wanted to make. The time you invest in getting that degree is a risk, but the reward will bring dividends. I've begun to realize that even when I risk something and lose, the lesson I learned from losing is invaluable and makes me better prepared for the next risk. So then, is it even possible for a risk to come back void?

TAKING ACTION

Now comes the real gear-shifting moment. My action plan began to filter through these three goals and guided my decisions. When COVID-19 hit and the monster truck industry shut down, all the "what" I did as a driver and brand ambassador went away. COVID-19 killed my "what."

I sat in my office and came up with an idea: what if I recorded motivational videos to offer to the Great Clips franchises to use for their salon teams? I filtered the idea through my three "who" goals. I had to have faith that Great Clips franchisees would want videos like this. Making the videos would force me to creatively develop appropriate talks that would deliver value to the salon teams. Spending money for the equipment and studio build-out at my home was risky. Plus, there was the risk of the time it would take to record and edit each video. This checked all three of my boxes—faith, creativity, and risk—so the answer to if I should do the motivational videos came easily.

I worked with the Monster Jam and Great Clips teams to develop a request form for franchisees, and I got started. I produced well over one hundred videos in no time, each ranging from three to ten minutes in length. I had built a unique product for franchisees to use to encourage their teams during a time in history that required a creative approach. Some of these videos were used on their private social media team pages, but most were played at their team training sessions and banquets during the few moments they could get together that year.

Two years later, I was still receiving motivational video requests from Great Clips franchisees. This venture also created a demand for the same type of content from our Monster Jam team to produce on the national level. If I had been focused on what I couldn't do when COVID-19 hit instead of who I wanted to become through that chapter of life, I never would have pushed myself into creating that type of value. Do you see how my best decisions are driven by who I want to become?

When I hear someone use the phrase "take action," it sounds like someone is saying, "do more." I've found that when I approach the demands of life with the commitment to become who I want to be, the decisions and actions tend to fall in place much easier and more quickly. So next time you struggle to understand why your college-aged nephew can't seem to move forward with his life or is making another head-scratching decision, just remember that the real problem may revolve around his confusion on *who* he wants to become in life. When was the last time you had that conversation with him? When was the last time you had that conversation with yourself?

WIPE YOUR WINDSHIELD

There's one main differentiator between NASCAR and Monster Jam. Each vehicle in NASCAR is identified mostly from the car's number on the side, while each Monster Jam truck—the truck itself—has its own persona. The Grave Digger truck isn't merely a brand with specific markings to identify it. The Grave Digger truck has a history of being *the* truck with *the* driver who creates the most spectacular carnage out on the track at a Monster Jam event. If you find yourself as the driver of this iconic truck, you better be ready to embody that "on the edge of out of control" persona.

Our lives have to be the same way. When you become passionate about the persona you want to carry into the world, you can steer it in the direction you want it to go. Your actions and mentality will adapt to it. If you see yourself as a person with just a number decaled on your side, you will know you're too focused on the *what* you're doing to be able to see the *who* you can become. For the record, you don't necessarily have to take more risks, have more faith, or be more creative to be the best version of yourself. You can be the adventurous thrill-seeker, the justice fighter, or even the rational consumer for that matter. Shifting your focus to *who* you want to become will be the secret to creating an action plan to make it all happen. That's how you'll shift out of the monotonous cycle of doing the same stuff every day, over and over, and expecting a miraculously different result.

It might be time for you to wipe off your windshield. Shift your focus. See yourself as the best version of yourself, and let's get you back in motion to live the life you've always wanted. I'll warn you that the most uncomfortable position to be in is when you first start moving from a standstill. That first step takes the most energy. Whether you've been stuck in neutral or living in fourth gear unable to find fifth, burnout is a real threat. The good news is that the next shift you make will handle that exact situation! Are you ready to start failing faster?

TUNE-UP

1. If you were a car, what kind would you be? Fast or slow? Gray or bright red? Old farm truck or two-door super car? Why?
2. In one word, how would people describe you today?
3. How would you like people to describe you when you're gone?

3

BURNOUT: 1ST GEAR

Fail Faster

Everyone loves a loud, tire-smoking burnout. Because our days are filled with watching cars operate in their intended, boring functions, we intensely watch when we see one that operates beyond the norm, where its performance is stretched past the simple use of safe transportation. We also wait in anticipation for the cops to show up at the parking lot where this burnout is unfolding in order to capture the drama on our phones so our social media followers can enjoy the festivities with us. We've got to get those "likes" and "shares."

I guess I should explain how to do a burnout, but I'll have to figure out where the disclaimer should go (cue publisher's increased blood pressure in 3 . . . 2 . . . 1 . . .). Performing a burnout in a car requires keeping it still while the driver spins the tires. This is typically done by "power braking," which consists of holding the brake pedal down while pressing the throttle pedal all the way to the floor. If a car has enough horsepower, the wheels will push through the brakes and start to spin the tires. Letting off the brake pedal will move the car forward while the tires fight to regain traction, usually producing a "screeching" sound.

I love doing burnouts. The key to doing a good one without getting caught is to produce so much smoke that the cops can't find you when they show up on the scene. Put it on your bucket list if you've never sat in a car doing a burnout (Ah! Here we go: "Don't try this at home. *You should only execute burnouts using a professional driver on a closed course!*" Nailed it.).

Pulling off a great burnout isn't just about pressing pedals, though. The real lesson comes when a driver learns how to feel the tires when they start to grab the asphalt again. He must decide when and how to let off the pedals as the traction comes back. Holding down the throttle pedal too long can cause the car to "fishtail" sideways out of control, but lifting off the throttle too early can result in damage to the motor. Rental car agencies hate professional race car drivers because their motto when traveling always seems to be, "Don't be gentle, it's a rental."

While car burnouts are exciting and entertaining, we all at one time or another experience our own form of life burnout. The movement of the spinning tires and laboring of the engine's rpm provide a good analogy for how burnout feels when the demands of life get to be too much. Like a nurse who just pulled her fourth 24-hour shift in a week for two months straight, or the entrepreneur still digging out of a pile of pandemic-related problems to turn his business back to cash flow-positive, everyone experiences this exhaustion at some point.

Back in the car, maybe you thought you could handle a burnout, only to find yourself fishtailing into a ditch. Life gets hard that way. But instead of waiting for the tow truck to come pull you out of the ditch, regaining your traction in life is a shift you can make if you know what gears are available to you. Surviving burnout in life requires three tactics: turning friction into function, hitting the right shift points, and learning when *not* to shift. Before we dive into these methods, let's get specific about what true life burnout looks like today.

CORPORATE BURNOUT

Burnout occurs when someone has too many demands and not enough solutions. The most challenging part of experiencing burnout is the feeling of failure that inevitably steals your self-confidence along the way. Your boss is expecting more. Your kids have more practices to get to yet come across as less than grateful at the dinner table. You hear about prioritizing mental health, but you assume that's code for getting time off. Deep down you worry more time off will only pile up the problems in your absence and quadruple the number of unread emails awaiting your return. The longer you accept burnout as the new normal, the less confident you will become that you're up for the task of meeting these increased and insurmountable demands.

The real travesty of this situation isn't the threat of failing to overcome these demands, but rather a change in your identity as a result. Your self-confidence stands to slowly erode with each heavy sigh when one of the plates you've been trying to spin falls to the ground. That's when you start to question if you have what it takes to manage the demand and ultimately find the solutions. The result: you buckle under the weight on your shoulders.

Corporate burnout doesn't occur only in an office building. Another word for *corporate* is *collective*. Any collective approach to an end goal can lead to the type of burnout I'm referring to. The classes you're taking comprise a collective approach between you and your teacher toward your education. Paying your bills out of your savings or checking account is a collective effort between you and the energy company to keep your lights on. Finishing your work projects so your company can hit its quarterly earnings is a collective effort between you and your colleagues to deliver on what you were hired to do.

What happens in these collective efforts, though, is that nobody is perfect. Your boss increases your workload without additional pay. Your teacher goes on vacation the week before your final paper is due and is unavailable to answer a critical question to help you complete the assignment. The energy company decides to add a fee to cover its losses from the pandemic, an unexpected expense for which you had no vote or control.

These corporate demands we experience are rarely easy to stomach, and they require us to get extremely creative to find solutions. Nobody likes living that way. We all try to find the path of least resistance, and we end up wanting to throw our hands up in desperation, ready to hit a big reset button on life. The good news is that just like that loud, smoke-filled burnout in your car, there are perspectives and techniques to help you overcome corporate burnout and get back on the right track with renewed excitement and engagement.

FAKE IDS

After I started working at the executive recruiting firm, I quickly became overwhelmed; it was a massive career change for me, more than I expected. I learned the firm's recruiting process and tried to understand how to correctly use the computer tracking system for candidates, and then I was given my first search. Because the firm was so busy, there was a new search project kicking off without any recruiters available to work on it. The senior vice president (SVP) in charge of the project had to look at the three new hires (me being one of them) and choose one of us to take the lead.

It just so happened to be a chief financial officer (CFO) search for a private equity firm's pet food manufacturing portfolio company. I knew zero about what a CFO did, what private equity was, or how pet food was manufactured. When I was told by Jim, the SVP for the project, that I had been tasked with this search, I immediately thought I had made a grave mistake by joining the firm. What happened to starting with a low-level search to gradually get my feet wet and then working my way up? On top of that, Jim was notoriously one of the strictest SVPs at the firm who militantly followed the recruiting process. Surely, I would be exposed as a fraud within a few weeks!

The demands of the search were intense—from the number of cold calls needing to be made, to entering data into the system, to hoping to prove to Jim I was the right choice for the project. It was a sink-or-swim situation. A common saying kept coming to my mind the first few days of the project: "Fake it 'til you make it!" But thinking of that made things worse for me. I sat down with Jim, nothing but a look of failure in my eyes, after my first day of calling CFOs to recruit them to our client's company. "I can't call these CFOs," I said. "I don't even know what they do! How am I supposed to convince them to uproot their lives?"

Jim said something that quickly banished the "fake it 'til you make it" mindset. "Bryce," he said, "when you believe you're the one they've been hoping would call with their dream career opportunity, the calls will become easy." It wasn't a question of skill or knowledge. It was a question of *identity*. I started a new saying, telling myself, "Believe it until I become it." That sounds a bit cheesy, but repeating it to myself over time (I still do) has allowed me to decide my identity and who I want to be rather than feeling like I'm faking something. I ended up finding multiple candidates for that CFO search, and we placed a talented executive at that pet food manufacturing company under the ninety-day targeted timeline.

That mindset "to believe it until I become it" has carried over to my career in Monster Jam, whether I'm racing behind the wheel of a 12,000-pound truck or hosting a Discovery Channel special event live on national television. I don't have to fake a smile or fake my activity because my identity drives my actions. I believed I was the recruiter with the golden opportunity someone had been waiting for. I believed I was the best choice to take over the Great Clips Mohawk Warrior's driver's seat in 2016, and I became the best fit to incubate the relationship between Great Clips as a new sponsor and Monster Jam. I believed I was a national television–caliber communicator until I became a national television host for that Discovery Channel special event. Envisioning and believing in who we are and who we can become allows us to have the confidence and clarity to do the work successfully.

FAILURE IS NOT FINAL

So here we go. It's time to grab hold of first gear and get your life back into motion. One specific secret has enabled me to fight through burnout and engage in the grind of life until I overcame obstacles. This secret is what gets me unstuck, out of neutral, and moving again when I feel like I am spinning out of control.

Have you ever been told, "Sometimes you win; sometimes you lose"? That little nugget is usually shared with a shrug of the shoulders and a sly grin from someone who is attempting to convince himself or herself that fate has caused them to become a victim of bad luck. Burnout creates an intense feeling of a lack of control, and phrases like that only intensify the idea that we're just in a canoe without a paddle, helplessly floating toward a massive waterfall.

During that first chief financial officer search project, I learned that success wasn't based on making that one call to an executive I would eventually end up placing at my client's company. Success was based on how quickly I could motor through the "nos." When I realized that an average search required around 125 pitch calls in which I shared the opportunity with an executive we had researched and targeted, my new focus became how quickly I could get through the 124 nos. I was so committed to moving past the nos that I began to get aggravated at the yeses.

That mindset created an atmosphere of hard work. It also allowed me to learn from each no. It got to the point where it was difficult to get to 124 nos on a project before having a solid slate of qualified candidates to move forward with. If we are going to get ourselves moving again, it is not a matter of finding our next success. Finding first gear means learning to fail faster. “You mean to fail more?” No, it is not about failing more or less. Every situation in life will have successes and failures, as well as obstacles, hurdles, curveballs, and flat tires. Committing to getting through the failures as quickly as possible gets you back into a mindset of taking action.

This failing faster gear carried over to driving a Monster Jam truck for me. At the end of the 2018 season, our tour members had a pizza party with a highlight video of the season. The videographer made a narrated blooper reel that included making fun of the number of attempts I had made that season at a “stoppie.” *Stoppie* is the term used to describe stopping the truck on the front two tires with the back of the truck in the air. The narrator said, “And Bryce

Kenny would go down in history as making the most failed stoppie attempts in the history of the sport!" Everyone found it hilarious; they'd had to endure watching me try this technical move repeatedly each weekend. It took me way too long to learn how to do it, although completing them now is second nature.

Back then, I knew if I had to attempt forty stoppies and fail at thirty-nine, I just had to fail at them as fast as I could until I got the feeling I needed as a driver to do them with my eyes closed (figure of speech, of course!). Now I'm able to balance a Monster Jam truck on the front tires for twenty-plus seconds and walk it up six-foot-tall dirt jumps in reverse with the back of the truck dangling in the air.

If I had been focused on success at the beginning, I wouldn't have survived the failures. My secret to failing fast is changing that old adage to, "Sometimes I win, sometimes I *learn*." Whether you're making new friends, building presentations at work, or forcing a Monster Jam truck to dance on its nose, the lessons you learn through failure will propel you to eventual successes. You just have to fail as fast as possible to get there as quickly as possible. Can you see how this shift in mindset actually produces a shift in your rate of activity?

TURNING FRICTION INTO FUNCTION

What are you supposed to *do* when you feel burned-out? Just suck it up and work harder? Definitely not. Oftentimes when I'm burned-out from work, traveling, or the demands of being a dad to three kids, my perspective can either be my greatest asset or my worst enemy. Burnouts in a car produce friction, and friction produces heat. But did you know that heating the tires makes the rubber sticky, which allows the tires to stay connected better to the track as it accelerates to high speeds? That's why cars do burnouts at a drag strip before they make a run. The friction has a function.

Like it or not, the burnout you experience in life also produces a certain stickiness to what you're striving toward. This stickiness creates an expectation that your efforts will eventually pay off, and oftentimes it gives you the endurance to see things through to the end. The only way your failure becomes fatal is when you quit. While this friction caused from being burned-out shouldn't be the goal you set for yourself, the perspective it can bring might just be the difference between quitting and overcoming hardship. What if this stickiness is preparing you for something greater in your future? Friction can feel scary and uncomfortable, but trust the fact that friction can equip you to see the positive outcomes and thus increases your expectations for potential results. I had to learn this tactic the hard way, and it almost cost me my relationship with my future wife.

In 2010, I was pursuing a lifelong dream of completing my Top Fuel drag-racing license. My whole world as I was growing up had been drag racing. When I wasn't weed eating the fence line at my grandfather's drag strip, I was racing our family's junior dragster every summer. I loved everything about drag racing; I had never been to any other motorsports event in my life (including a monster truck event) until I was in my twenties. I was finally pursuing my dream, working seven different jobs to pay the bills, yet I was getting my teeth kicked in every step of the way. After a few years of beating my head against the wall, I was burned-out with very little hope of making a race car driving career happen.

McKenzie and I had been dating for four years at that point, and she was starting to wonder if my racing ambitions would ever turn into something that would allow us to get married and start our life together. I'll admit that I had no intention of letting anything get in the way of my chance of becoming a professional race car driver. I was running toward my dream so hard that I was pushing away the people in my life who cared about me. The problem was that my Top Fuel drag racing ambitions weren't going as I had hoped, and I was more physically and mentally exhausted than I'd ever been in my life.

McKenzie and I were not in a good place either. After my final Top Fuel race that year, everything came to a head. I was tired, lost, and angry. I felt like an inadequate failure who had chased a dream reserved for people who were smarter, more charming, and more determined than me. Not to mention, I still lived with my parents so I could put more money into my racing dream. I sat in my car in the driveway at 3:00 a.m. crying my eyes out. I had more snot running out of my nose than an English bulldog had drool hanging out its mouth.

Feelings of failure and inadequacy are quite dangerous because they can make you agree with them about who you are inside, and their lies can take years to undo. Lies like, "I'm not enough. I'm a failure. I'm not smart enough. I'm ashamed." I wasn't feeling sorry for myself. I was *burned-out*. Expired. Not living the way I was designed to live. The demands were far greater than any solutions I could find. I didn't know where to turn next or what move to make. It just wasn't working. I needed help.

I had a mentor at the time named Gary, and he came out to that last race to support me. He saw me suffering silently after the night ended abruptly from bad weather, which cost my team money because we couldn't complete all the race passes down the track that we were contracted to make. I sat with Gary a few days after that last race, and he said to me, "You're keeping so many plates spinning in the air that some are starting to fall and break. You can't be all things to all people, and you need to decide what's most important to you. If you don't prioritize things, you're going to start losing them. You have to get your house in order if you ever want to be in a position to make a difference."

It was like Gary saw straight through me. He then asked me if I was willing to lose McKenzie over my racing aspirations. I immediately said no. I realized she was the only thing in my life I wasn't willing to lose. He encouraged me to give up the things I wanted now in racing for what I wanted most. Two weeks later, I asked McKenzie to marry me.

The moral of this story is that ever since I showed her that she was more important to me than my career, she's never felt the need to ask me to give it up. She was the first person to tell me to go drive for Monster Jam when the opportunity arose. She's my biggest supporter now as my wife and mom of our three amazing kids, even when my travel situation gets incredibly difficult to manage. I've proven to her that I'd give up everything if she asked me to, therefore she doesn't feel the need to ask me to do that. The intense *friction* we experienced back in 2010 served as a *function* that has allowed for a deeper partnership ever since in our life. It wasn't easy to go through at the time, but now I'm thankful for the burnout we endured back then.

HITTING THE SHIFT POINTS

Now that you're getting better at understanding burnouts, let's take it to the next level. Most of the time you'll start your burnout in first gear, pushing the wheels through the brakes as I described earlier. When you get to the point where your engine is laboring a lot in first gear, you need to shift into second. That will bring down the engine rpm and increase your tire speed, which will create even more smoke.

However, you can't spin your tires forever. At this point you'll want to slowly lift your left foot off the brake pedal so the car begins to move forward. The tires will fight to regain traction and pull you along the road. And yes, you guessed it, the same technique applies to being burned-out in life. Sometimes all you need to do is shift into a different gear to start reengaging yourself and getting back on the right track.

As you work your way through the gears in the following chapters, you'll learn not only what the gears themselves look like when applied to life, but also when to shift into each one.

The best transmission in the world is useless when it's just sitting in neutral, even if it's attached to the most powerful engine. Learning when to shift into the right gear is critical to regaining traction.

For instance, sometimes I need to shift into being purpose driven when I'm battling self-doubt. When I'm struggling with the culture of Monster Jam after being on tour with the same people for six months, I have to shift into being built for others and become focused on serving people. When I walk in my front door exhausted after traveling for a week, I have to shift into the mindset of wanting to make memories with my loved ones instead of withdrawing to my bedroom to check my social media and mentally unplug. At my core, I've determined these beliefs are true. I have to hit my shift points into these gears at the right time so they guide my decisions and help me regain traction when I feel like I'm spinning my wheels. And that's exactly what the following chapters will give you.

LEARN WHEN *NOT* TO LIFT!

Occasionally a situation arises when all the chaos happening in our environment makes us want to lift our foot off the throttle and disengage. We think we can reset and start over in a safer way. However, sometimes the only way over an obstacle is to mash your foot on the throttle pedal and push through it. I've been in situations in a Monster Jam truck where that was my only option.

When I competed in my very first Monster Jam World Finals in 2017, the track designer placed a water obstacle on top of one of the dirt mounds on the track. It was a makeshift pond probably twenty feet by twenty feet with a fountain. During my freestyle run, I approached a jump that sent me hurling through the air and into the side of a nearby jump, causing me to tumble sideways toward the pond. I turned the front tires to attempt to save the truck from rolling over, gave it some throttle in hopes the giant tires would find enough grip in the dirt to maintain momentum, and landed back on all four tires right into that pond. The fans went absolutely crazy and started cheering so loud I could hear them over the engine noise from my truck.

My only thought at that moment was, "Bryce, whatever you do, don't get this 12,000-pound Monster Jam truck stuck in a foot of water!" I slammed my foot on the throttle, unleashed the 1,500-horsepower motor to give the tires their best chance at continuing my momentum out of there, and sent that pond water sailing thirty feet into the air. I destroyed the fountain, but I quickly got out of it and continued the rest of my freestyle run accompanied by a thunderous roar from the crowd.

Spinning my tires in that pond did not create any stickiness to produce traction. If I had shifted into another gear, I wouldn't have gotten out. My only choice was to throttle out of the pond. Sometimes an environment is not conducive to traction, and your best bet is to keep your foot on the throttle until you move through it. If you're experiencing burnout in life and your environment is the culprit, I doubt the answer is to take a formulaic approach to getting out of it. Adopt this motto and keep it in your back pocket for those instances when nothing else will get you out of your feeling of being burned-out: "When in doubt, throttle out!"

REGAINING TRACTION

The most important question I could ask someone experiencing burnout in life is, "What do you want *most?* versus, What do you want *now*?" If it feels like you're spinning your wheels and can't seem to regain traction in your home, school, job, or any other part of life, maybe you're looking for an answer to the wrong question. Maybe you're so focused on what you want *now* that you've forgotten about what you want *most*. I can confidently say that I have always been prepared to do whatever it takes to make my life count, but I have *not* always been willing to give up the things that I needed to in my life to find real traction.

If investing two hours a day to learn everything about the area you want to pursue was all it took to realize your dream, would you give up binge-watching the new season of your favorite show? Sometimes you might think, "I'd travel seven days a week to put food on the table" (and I believe it is our duty to provide for the ones we love). But what if you're experiencing burnout because of the job you think you have to do, rather than realizing that giving up the job with seven days of travel is what will keep your family together?

When you're willing to give up the little kingdom you've built for yourself, you begin to build a support system unlike anything you could imagine with the people in your life who need you most. In 2010, I stepped away from my pursuit of being a professional driver and became the hero my future wife needed by getting our house in order. Being the hero for other people doesn't mean you will never experience burnout. Being the hero means you're willing to regain traction at all cost.

Turning friction into function, hitting your shift points at the right time, and having the mindset of "When in doubt, throttle out" might make the difference in going from burnout to all-out to make an impact on your world. Once you shift into your first gear of failing faster, you start to realize the value you can bring others along the way. Now that you see the value you can bring, you're ready to make the critical shift of choosing to believe that your efforts will actually turn into real results toward living the life you've always wanted! Are you ready to make the next shift?

TUNE-UP

1. What do you want now?
2. What do you want most?
3. What do you need to give up to get the thing you want most?

4

PRESSURE: 2ND GEAR

Choose to Believe Rather Than Doubt

Driving a monster truck is insanely fun. But in 2017, I would have been hard-pressed to describe my experience as fun when I found myself in a high-pressure situation as the driver for the newly sponsored Great Clips Mohawk Warrior truck. This happened during a time when the monster truck community, my sponsors, and I had high expectations to perform, and it turned out to be too much for me.

I wanted to drive like a veteran, but I was still a rookie. The more I wanted to win, the tenser I got, and the worse I drove. Instead of allowing myself to learn, I was too focused on results. I started to doubt myself and my abilities to the point where a medical scare landed me in an emergency room in Albuquerque, New Mexico. There was no question that the stress I was feeling, much of it self-imposed, and my medical emergency were connected.

It was my first season competing in a series where we drove Monster Jam trucks, side-by-sides, and ATVs. My failure of not finding big sponsorship money in drag racing years earlier had stuck with me and contributed to my wanting to deliver for a sponsor in a big way. This felt like my shot at redemption. I couldn't let everyone down.

The night before my ER visit, I had a crash in a competition that rang my bell a bit. It didn't look like a hard-hitting crash from outside the truck. I was competing in a technical skills event where drivers try to pull off their best tricks with the truck on two wheels. I hit an obstacle to send the truck up vertically into a "sky wheelie" and over rotated just enough to land on the back of the chassis with the nose still in the air. Staring at the bottom of the arena's jumbotron out of my windshield, I felt the truck falling backward off the obstacle. The first part of the truck to hit the ground was the roll cage right above my head. In case you're wondering, there is no suspension on that part of the truck.

I lay upside down, patiently waiting on the "crane of

shame" to come flip me back over. Adding insult to injury, I was aggravated that I had crashed and damaged the truck again. I couldn't shake off the feeling of defeat for the rest of the night from my mishap. It affected me somehow in a manner I had never experienced.

When I awoke the next morning, I felt a beating in my chest that wouldn't subside, and I self-diagnosed it as nerves. I was extremely frustrated at that point in the season, and my crew chief was miffed at my inability to avoid damage from crashes as well. We were splintering. We were bleeding as we grew closer to the finish line each weekend. It wasn't a winning formula.

When I got to the stadium, I was so mentally fatigued that I probably looked like a walking zombie to the rest of our team. I got a call from my boss at Monster Jam; he was exasperated that I had crashed again and caused damage to the truck's fiberglass body. That phone call took any remaining wind out of my sails for the day. Feeling defeated, I planned to suck it up and get through the day.

Thankfully, our event manager knew something was wrong just by looking at and listening to me, and he made me go see the medics at the stadium. They did some tests and took my blood pressure, which was 170 over 110—a lot higher than that of a healthy person. The medical folks were alarmed and suggested I immediately go to the hospital. Their demeanor freaked me out more than the numbers did. Ten minutes later, while I was trying to decide what to do, they retook my blood pressure and found that it had spiked to 200 over 130—the danger zone. They told me those were numbers typically seen in someone having a heart attack. I thought for a split second, "Could I be having one? Could this kill me?"

I called my dad, whose voice has always been the first I want to hear when I'm in a medical situation. I told him what was happening, and his first response was to comically ask, "Does the stadium happen to be selling wine by chance?" We were essentially in a horse arena at a fairground, so his proposed cause was preposterous. "No, Dad, walking up to the concourse and asking if anyone is selling wine isn't an option right now," I responded, annoyed. But he said, "Bryce, you're probably having a panic attack. You have to find a way to slow your heart rate and try to calm down. You're going to be OK, son."

For some reason, hearing him tell me that made me feel like I had some level of control over the situation. He told me to get an ice pack on my chest and on my neck, and to lie flat on my back with my eyes closed. Within ten minutes, I felt the pressure start to subside. I was fighting the idea of leaving in an ambulance because that seemed too dramatic. Looking back, I should've immediately let the medics take me to the hospital. I ended up calming my heart rate enough so that, about an hour later, I felt stable enough to let a competing driver named Cole Venard drive me to the hospital, where they ran some tests to see if I had any deeper health problems going on. After a few hours of precautionary testing, I left the hospital with normal blood pressure and headed back to the hotel. I've never had a massive blood pressure spike like that since.

Realizing what caused the health scare allowed me to stay calm enough to address it—without any wine, I might add. But this whole medical situation gave me a new appreciation for people who deal with panic attacks and severe anxiety. Handling pressure isn't as easy as simply shifting perspective. I believe we must choose to believe that we are going to make it through any problem. For me, hearing my dad tell me he believed I would be OK made me believe it too. But there have been times in my life when making the difficult choice to believe rather than doubt is easier said than done. My earliest lesson on this subject came in the heart of a remote cave system in Kentucky.

LIGHTS OUT

Growing up, I had four uncles (my mom's brothers). Their names are Mike, Dan, Chris, and Aaron, and each of them had hung the moon in my eyes. All I cared about back then was looking cool around them. My uncles were all fun-loving, accomplished guys and adrenaline junkies, their ranks collectively consisting of chiropractors, mechanics, racers, and paintballers. Mike was my Top Fuel crew chief and managed the day-to-day for the entire team for years; my dream of driving a Top Fuel car never would have happened without him. Dan became a close friend during my adult years, and even now we restore old cars together as an excuse to talk about our lives and our next real estate deals. Chris always believed in me, and I honestly cannot think of a negative word he ever spoke to me. Aaron was the wild uncle who somehow found time to have fun and make memories with his much-younger nephews.

When I was ten years old, Chris and Aaron concocted an adventure for my brother Richard and me. They took us caving in Jackson County, Kentucky, an area known for its many caves worthy of spelunking. I had never been caving, but if my uncles thought it would be fun, I was in.

We didn't go to a famous or well-known cave, though. I had envisioned a large opening with lots of people going in and out and taking pictures. The one we went to had a small opening in backwoods Kentucky, and I didn't see another soul. We went in, and the caves were much bigger inside than I had expected from the small opening outside. We started checking out the small streams as well as the stalagmites and stalactites. We had been there for about an hour and continued to go deeper into the cave system, well past the point where any outside light was available, when I noticed my uncles growing quieter with each minute that passed. Still, we continued onward, albeit more slowly.

Another thirty minutes or so into our adventure, and I thought we must be almost to the end of this cave system, but the tones of my uncles' voices did not sound encouraging. They seemed to be getting nervous and started to debate which way to go. I had been walking around every corner we came to acting like Indiana Jones looking for the ark of the covenant until I realized something was wrong with our adventure. Pretty soon, my uncles were in full-blown panic mode. We were officially lost. The more we tried to find a way out, the more lost we got. We hadn't seen another person.

My uncles decided to conserve battery power on the flashlights by having only one turned on at a time, and that was when I really started to freak out. Only having one flashlight to light the way slowed us down even more because it was suddenly much harder to watch our footing through the difficult terrain. We hadn't brought food because this wasn't supposed to be a long adventure. The plan was to check out some caves and be back for lunch. A dinnertime return seemed more likely at this point.

We continued for three more hours. Around every corner I could hear the disappointment in my uncles' sighs when we didn't see daylight. My only hope of surviving was tied to the battery life in the flashlights. As long as we had light, I had all the hope in the world that we'd eventually find our way out. That hope was starting to fade, however, right about the time our last working flashlight started to flicker.

Suddenly, we heard a faint noise that eventually became a voice and a flashlight. We had found a small group of cavers, the first people we'd seen since our trek began. They were well supplied with headlamps and maps of the cave system. They heard the panic in our voices and immediately joked, "You boys must be some of them city slickers!" They told us how to get out, and I have not been back into a cave since.

The most valuable thing I learned in the cave that day was that believing daylight waits around the next corner is a *choice*, no matter how dark and disorienting life can seem. That experience taught me never to doubt that something good can happen. I used to think that believing in good things was just an attitude, but a positive attitude tends to follow this *choice* to first believe that the solution to a problem is on the way.

MAKING THE CHOICE

When I had my intense anxiety attack in Albuquerque, my problem wasn't a hyper-competitive attitude or eating bad chicken the night before. I was doubting that I had made the right decision to go full-time with Monster Jam and leave my corporate career behind. I was doubting that this was all going to work out for the better. By doubting my future, I was subconsciously trying to protect myself from disappointment. I spent so much time doubting that I wouldn't have known what to do if something positive had come my way.

Admittedly, there's something about sitting in an emergency room that causes a person to take stock of their life and examine the road they chose that led to their predicament. I realized I might not have consciously chosen to doubt my career decisions, but I *would* have to consciously choose to believe in good outcomes and possibilities if I were going to turn things around long-term.

Whether you're suffering from a medical issue, stuck deep in a cave system, or simply trying to figure out if you can pay all your bills this month, choosing to believe that your solution is waiting on you gives you the clarity and focus to take the steps to make it happen. Remember: it takes just as much effort to doubt as to believe. So don't waste your energy. Believing is a *choice*, just like doubting is a choice. We better make the right one.

TOO MUCH PRESSURE

It might sound odd, but one of the best lessons I learned about choosing to believe in good outcomes while pursuing my goals came from a mental approach to driving a Monster Jam truck. My desire to perform, entertain, and win in front of thousands of fans in a stadium has always been extremely high. Desire is great, but there is a limit, and going beyond it is unhealthy. We sometimes want something so badly that we unwittingly create anxiety that prevents us from seeing our desire come to fruition.

For instance, on most weekends when I travel, I have to wake up at 3:00 a.m. to catch a flight to come back home. I might not get back to the hotel after a Monster Jam event until 11:00 p.m., and then I quickly set my alarm for 2:45 a.m. to head to the airport the following morning. "OK, if you fall asleep right now, you'll get almost four hours of sleep. That's totally fine," I'll convince myself. Then I start counting sheep and lie as still as possible as I try to doze off. But I'm unsuccessful. I peer over at the clock that now says 12:15 a.m. "No big deal. You'll be tired, but if you fall asleep right now, you'll still get a couple hours of sleep," I reason. Deep down, I know that I *have* to fall asleep or I'll be a walking zombie later. The harder I try to fall asleep, the less likely I am to hit that dream state. I eventually learned through the years to try to trick myself into thinking I don't want to fall asleep. Maybe it's some form of reverse psychology, but I tell myself that I honestly don't care if I lie there all night and never fall asleep. Somehow that always makes me go right to sleep.

Anxiety forms when we try to force an outcome we can't control, and it prevents us from obtaining that desired outcome. The more I want to win in a Monster Jam truck, the worse I drive. Desire can lead to effort, but we have to live in this gear of choosing to believe if we want to become the best version of ourselves.

We can be focused on who we want to become (as I've discussed in earlier chapters), but we cannot control the results from our efforts. We must learn how to choose to believe that positive results will come. This allows us to control the controllables and prevents us from only focusing on the results. We can only control our actions and attitudes, so we have to learn to trust that the results will take care of themselves.

Imagine holding Jell-O in the palm of your hand. In this illustration, Jell-O represents the outcome you desire most. The harder you try to control everything to achieve that outcome, the more you're going to squeeze it through your fingers and have it fall out of your grip. If you focus on believing your actions will be adequate to get you to the best result possible instead of focusing on the outcomes you ultimately cannot control, you'll find a critical gear in achieving goals you never knew you had.

TURNING BELIEFS INTO RESULTS

At some point, belief always drives behavior. When I was stuck in that cave, my belief that daylight would be around the next corner drove my behavior to keep walking after three hours despite a thought in the back of my mind that we might be in serious trouble. If I had believed I were going to die, I would've just curled up in a ball in the corner and starved to death. Since I believed we would eventually find our way out, my behavior followed.

In life, when you believe in a negative outcome, you produce negative behavior. Thankfully, when you choose to believe in a positive one, your actions start to align with the behavior that will produce positive results. Had I believed in a negative outcome in Albuquerque during my medical scare, my blood pressure might have kept climbing to the point where I would have had a heart attack. Once I believed in the positive outcome and that I could lower my blood pressure by twenty minutes of deep breathing and refocusing, positive results came.

When you apply this belief strategy to your life, the simplicity of it is profound. If a person believes animals are innocent and deserve to be protected, she probably isn't holding dog fights in her backyard. If someone believes humans have immense value, he probably isn't out there hurting or murdering people. If you believe there's a chance you could be involved in a car wreck on the way to work, you're probably going to take those extra three seconds to fasten your seat belt once you're inside your car. Our actions are driven by what we believe. If you're struggling to nail down your set of beliefs, look at your day-to-day actions and follow the breadcrumbs backward.

Two foundational questions seem to form most of our beliefs: "Why am I here?" and "Do I have what it takes?" If you struggle to answer those questions and are reluctant to expend the mental effort to decide, look at your behaviors.

For example, some people use other people solely for their own gain. That sounds harsh, but we all know someone who seems to befriend others only when that person wants something from them. That person believes (maybe even subconsciously) that they exist to climb the ladder and protect themselves at all costs (survival of the fittest). Alternatively, if someone feels deep down that they're not an accident and have a sense of purpose, chances are good they will enjoy serving others, leaving an impact, and protecting their family (if they have one). They'll probably leave this world and society in better shape than they found it. The beliefs they hold have driven their actions their entire life; you and I are no different. If you don't like your actions, it might be time to look under your hood to determine what you believe. When you're hyperfocused on outcomes you haven't attained, your resentment toward life and those around you will likely build up so much that you start having engine failure, so to speak. Shifting to a mode of letting your beliefs drive you is critical to getting back on the right track.

SETTING A WINNING VISION

I'm not suggesting that your desire to win is unimportant. Having a target or a vision for your life is critical. Without vision, you would be aimlessly racing around without a finish line. I believe that setting a great, attainable target is belief-based, not outcome-based. You should reverse engineer it. The most effective visions come from the most solid beliefs.

When I dreamed of a career as a professional driver, my original plan was to succeed in drag racing. I didn't care about any other form of motorsports. I've still never been to a NASCAR or Formula 1 race. As I said before, the first time I attended a Monster Jam event was after I first spoke to the company about possibly driving a truck. It turns out my transition from drag racing to Monster Jam was a brilliant one, but it never would've happened if I had remained committed to my original career goal. If nothing but a career in drag racing had been acceptable, I would have unknowingly limited myself.

Believing I was meant for *motorsports in general* ultimately drove my behavior to change my path toward a career with Monster Jam. My belief drove my behavior to go train in a truck, and then it drove my decision to leave corporate America for a career with Monster Jam. These days my belief drives my behavior to try to make the biggest impact on the motorsports community that I can. When the belief was right, my behaviors aligned. I was then primed to set the huge vision of utilizing my platform to change as many lives as possible. Most importantly, I've been able to stay committed to seeing it happen since my actions are driven by my beliefs.

When you can see what you want with your eyes closed as clearly as what you see with your eyes open, your whole world changes. I'm convinced we're the only creatures on earth with an imagination, yet some of us forget how to use it by the time we get into high school. A good place to start is with the age-old high school guidance counselor question: "If you could get paid $1 million to do anything on earth, what would it be?" When the answer to a question like that is based on a set of beliefs instead of an arbitrary outcome, we're able to clearly envision a finish line that we can stay committed to for the long haul. It also becomes way more difficult for doubt to creep in along the way. Let's make that shift toward believing in a positive result so we can become confident in doing the hard work to make it happen. Next, let's check our fuel gauge and empty our tank in third gear!

TUNE-UP

1. When was the last time you felt overwhelmed by an unknown outcome in life?
2. Would you describe yourself as optimistic or pessimistic? Which of those words would others use to describe you? Why?
3. What is the "Jell-O" in your palm for which you need to start believing positively? What action can you take today that will be a step toward seeing that result come to fruition?

5

THRASH: 3RD GEAR

Empty the Tank

There's something in motorsports called "the thrash" that occurs in the pit area involving the race car. In Top Fuel, the thrash takes place between each round of racing when a team completely rebuilds their 10,000-horsepower engine in under seventy minutes to be ready for the next round. Fans pack NHRA pit areas at races across the country to watch this phenomenon take place. It really is that amazing and enthralling.

In Monster Jam, a team might have twenty-five minutes to swap out a transmission to get a truck back in a freestyle competition if the driver had obliterated it in a collision. Surviving a thrash is the difference between a good team and a great one. You never really know what you have in a team until it's faced with one of these sink-or-swim situations where everyone's back is against the wall.

The thrash, for me, has always been the best part about motorsports. Something is so calming about the chaos, as weird as that might seem. Don't get me wrong. I'd prefer not to have my machine's survival threatened for the remainder of a race by damage, but it's also a quick reminder of how insanely cool it is that we get to push this equipment past its limits at times.

I had a season in Monster Jam where I didn't feel confident that my team was capable of surviving a thrash, which cautioned me to drive more conservatively. Other seasons, I knew my team was up to the task if we suffered damage, and knowing that usually gave me the freedom to push the limits each weekend. How to survive a thrash cannot be taught, only experienced. A team that can thrash has endured being thrown into those situations enough times to know how to focus, communicate, and work with one another to skillfully tackle and finish. It really is a work of art and a symphony of its own when pulled off without a hitch.

If you're going to shift into your full potential, this is a gear you must find in your life. No matter the situation you have to endure, learning how to thrash is a critical component to finishing your race.

EMPTYING THE TANK

We've all been guilty of letting our car's gas gauge get below a quarter tank, especially when we're hoping to fill up at our favorite station in town with the lowest price per gallon. But how often do we actually run out of gas? We're so in tune with how much gas our car has left, but we often forget about our own physical, mental, and emotional tanks that become depleted as life demands resources from us each day. Emptying the tank isn't about a race car maximizing its resources for a checkered flag. It's about being aware of the status of our internal tanks so we can press through the extra demands of life while also understanding when we need to refill ourselves.

I was once brought in to speak at a men's retreat for a church in the northeast. Having a professional monster truck driver tasked to encourage a group of men who wanted to shift into their full potential was a great fit for their "Way of the Warrior"-themed weekend. The retreat's organizers asked me to prepare for a total of seven sessions over the course of the three-day weekend. I knew it would be difficult to get enough material ready, but those are the moments I always imagined would be available to me with a career in motorsports—the platform in my dreams that I spoke of earlier. I thrashed out content for three months leading up to the weekend and went into it with all the energy I could muster. By Sunday afternoon, I was wiped out. I still had one more session to go that evening before flying out early Monday morning. Before I headed back for the final session, I called McKenzie to check in.

"How are you feeling?" she asked.

"I'm exhausted, but I've got enough in the tank to finish tonight at least. I'm fine knowing I'm coming home tomorrow and will have a few days to refuel this week," I answered. She wasn't buying it. Had it not been for shot gunning two energy drinks about an hour before I took the stage for the final time that evening, I probably wouldn't have made it through. Those drinks kicked in hard, though, and the final session was a victory lap of sorts for our entire group.

The secret I've found to emptying my fuel tank through these taxing moments in life is to know how I will refill myself afterward. Introverts need alone time to recharge. Type A personalities need to accomplish something or see real results from their efforts. Some people need to feel safe and secure before they make the next move or take the next risk. Whether it's relationships, results, alone time, a good book, prayer, organizing your calendar, or some other form of refueling, understanding what refills your tank is the number-one priority before making the shift to emptying yourself. Once I realized that time with my family, a good supper, sleep, and doing something where I can see real-time results—such as sweeping out the garage—refuels my tank, I no longer hesitated to empty myself in my pursuit of building my motorsports platform as big as possible.

Imagine a race car driver circling the track with no clue where the pit lane is located. That driver wouldn't race as hard if he didn't know where to refuel when the tank got low. He would conserve. That's how we approach life far too often. When you know where to refuel, you need not be afraid to consume every drop in the race. Knowing where your pit stop will be and when you need to pull over gives you the confidence to keep going.

MAKE THE PIT STOP

Before we make that stop, let me explain something about the world in which I operate and how it applies to this chapter. The motorsports industry today is trying to provide value the same way it did in 1988, when only a decal on the side of a race car was needed to carry the clout to convince a company to invest millions of marketing dollars in that race team. Those were the days, but times and marketing tactics have changed considerably. That former thinking doesn't provide the same return on investment that it used to, and innovation is needed, which is why one of my goals as a Monster Jam driver is to work harder for sponsors than any other driver out there. I want to add so much value and return on investment for brands that I change what it means in the motorsports industry to be a brand ambassador. Doing so often requires me to completely empty my physical and mental fuel tanks in pursuit of that goal.

My critics judge me for wanting this more than wanting to win a world championship. "Maybe if you approached your driving with the same vigor as you do your partnerships, you'd win a lot more," some say. I don't deny that. The problem is that they weren't with me for the years in drag racing when I walked out of office buildings with my binder full of sponsorship proposals in hand after suffering yet another rejection. On one such occasion, as my shiny dress shoes hit the parking lot and I fumbled pulling the keys out of my pocket, I said out loud, "If someone would just give me a chance, I'd show them what I could do!"

Nobody would take a chance on me for the first five years I tried to make my dream happen. Those memories of rejection created an overwhelming feeling of gratitude when I came off the stage in 2018 after speaking at my first

Great Clips national convention. Three thousand franchise managers and stylists were in the audience, and I gave them all I had in my speech. Quite honestly, there was very little expectation for me as their newly sponsored Monster Jam driver. So when I got up there with an eight-minute speaking window, I had to make as much impact as I could. Luckily, my passion didn't have to be manufactured. That passion was fueled by my past failures and resulted in my resolve to thrash in, determined—once they gave me the opportunity—to give a brand more value than they signed up for.

I'm so grateful for the chance to live out my passion with a partner like Great Clips. Since that day, we've done both live speaking engagements and hundreds of virtual videos for the 700 franchisees and 30,000 stylists in the Great Clips system. After that first speaking engagement, one conversation with someone at Monster Jam stuck with me.

"We had no idea you were a speaker," they said. "Did you build that speech, or did you wing it?"

After telling them I had spent many hours writing, prepping, and practicing the eight-minute talk, they just looked at me surprised, with raised eyebrows. My effort was based on a desire to empty my fuel tank instead of portraying myself as some motivational guru speaker. I reminded my Monster Jam team that there was a time not long before when no one was asking me to speak or motivate teams. I wanted that invitation, and I had been waiting years for someone to give me the opportunity. I wasn't about to waste it. I would've spent a thousand hours on the talk if I'd needed to.

I do have one secret to share, though: I'm not addicted to the spotlight. I'm addicted to the prep for my speaking engagements. The level of self-reflection and vulnerability cuts me open every time I prepare, and those hundred hours leading up to an engagement make me a better version of myself. It is much easier for me to shift into a gear of "emptying my fuel tank," or thrashing, when I know the result is the type of person I want to become: a man relentlessly committed to unlocking the best version of myself, while helping other people do the same along the way.

My family is quite uncomfortable when I tell them about how I failed in my drag racing dream. I explain to them, however, that failure has built the steely resolve in me to want to empty my fuel tank in everything I do. I got my butt kicked so badly in my pursuit of a professional career in drag racing that I understand the fragility of my career in professional motorsports today. Emptying my fuel tank in pursuit of my dream is rooted in experiencing failure. If

I'm not constantly thinking about how to bring value to other people and strategically delivering that value in a way that impacts others, the opportunity disappears. Everything in life has a season. The best partnerships in business are built upon that relentless commitment to bring value and understand our window of time to make an impact together. We can't waste it.

ONE MORE LAP

One weekend in Anaheim, California, I crashed in a race against Grave Digger. I won the battle but lost the war. I caused about $60,000 in damage from a single crash after crossing the finish line sideways, causing my truck to cartwheel. It was a wild ride! But I destroyed all four of my front shocks and most of the drivetrain on the front half of the truck as a result. Sometimes a truck is damaged so severely that it requires days to repair, not minutes. This was one of those instances.

As our "crane of shame" recovery equipment towed my truck off the track and up the ramp to our pit area in the parking lot, the broken drive shaft made the worst screeching sound I've ever heard as it dragged against the concrete the entire way. Our team evaluated the damage without touching the truck, knowing it would be a project to tackle during the week. I was forced to watch the rest of the event from the sidelines. The worst part was that an error I made had caused the damage. Hitting the race lane crossing the finish line crooked wasn't the mistake; my decision to turn the front tires into the dirt as I landed caused the front end to buckle underneath the 12,000-pound chassis. When jumping a Monster Jam truck twenty feet in the air sideways, I now know to turn the front tires slightly away from the ground to prevent this cartwheel effect. I learned that the hard way.

Moments like that are the hardest to tolerate as a driver, knowing that my wrong decision caused the entire team to suffer. Our team would've loved the opportunity to thrash that night to get us back out on the track, but the damage was beyond a same-day repair. As bad as the situation was, we had to switch our focus to getting the truck ready for the next weekend. Thinking about how we were missing out on critical season points by being sidelined for the rest of the event wouldn't help us accomplish anything. We chose to focus on the positive note that at least we managed to beat Grave Digger in racing!

Life sometimes throws us situations that feel irreparable. In those moments we sit back, unable to speak, with both hands on our heads in exasperation. Maybe you lost a job, received a bad medical diagnosis, or experienced the loss of a loved one. You can't see a clear path forward. In those moments, you tend to lose focus of the small things, and your grip on progress seems to loosen. In sports, this would be called bungling the "fundamentals"—the core techniques that allow a competitor to perform consistently at a higher level. When we get tired, the first thing we skip over are the fundamentals. When the race of life throws you the hard stuff, you must focus on the fundamentals. Send that next email. Make that next sales call. Set that next appointment. Coordinate picking up your kid from school; be there ahead of time. Study for that next class.

When you feel like you're losing the race, you can't think about the finish line. You must focus on making the fastest lap possible on the next go-round. Don't allow the finish line to overwhelm you. Find a second wind to go one more lap. Having a sustained "one more lap" mentality can get you through the most grueling thrashes and propel you to finish the race.

BECOME A FINISHER

There's confusion in our society concerning the "never quit" mantra that finds itself in some form or phrase on bumper stickers and T-shirts. Truth be told, there are quite a few things I've technically quit:

- Top Fuel drag racing
- Cryptocurrency day trading after I realized I didn't have the risk appetite to figure out what made it go up or down
- Restoring a 1985 Chevy Silverado K10
- Restoring bourbon barrels
- Learning to play the drums
- My town's parks and rec advisory board
- Collegiate soccer

We all have things we've given up on. It's hard for me to admit I quit Top Fuel, because I feel like I finished that chapter only for the time being, and yet it turned out to be the right move for my family. As for soccer, I got injured in college and was unable to continue playing. The parks and rec advisory board position became comical after a few years of wasting an hour each month attending meetings where we discussed the upcoming grass cutting at one of the local parks. I tried to learn snare drum rudiments for two days and realized I wasn't interested in banging on the single snare drum my mom bought me after I convinced her to let me learn how to become a drummer. I lost interest in the 1985 Silverado and had a plan to refinish only five bourbon barrels anyways. I admit, lots of rationalization occurred on my part there.

The older I get, the more opportunities come my way. I don't succeed on every investment and haven't capitalized on every decision. But I find an immense amount of peace by focusing on *finishing*. Sometimes you need to quit spending time on things that don't move you toward the end goal of becoming the person you want to become. But there's also wisdom in learning how to become better positioned to finish, because life isn't always about either winning or quitting altogether—sometimes, it's about finishing.

Stu Weber wrote in his book *Tender Warrior*, "Finishing is a rare and valuable commodity. Completing the task. Staying till the final whistle. Driving the last nail. Never walking away. No pulling back. No drifting. No waffling. What this world needs are a few more finishers. What your family and mine need are finishers." Weber suggests that to be a finisher, four qualities must be present:

1. A clear eye for the goal, *a focused pursuit*. Call it vision.
2. A strong heart to get there, *an undivided heart*. Call it single-mindedness.
3. A little fire in the belly, *a driving intensity*. Call it determination.
4. A certain confidence. *A biblical optimism*. Call it faith.

I'd be lying if I said I was the best example of how to properly finish every race you run. Truthfully, my inspiration for learning to finish well comes from people I've met along the way. How does a teenage kid going through cancer process that his life could end? What becomes his focus when he tries to come to terms with the fact that his days are numbered? I learned from a warrior named Christian what being a finisher truly looks like.

CHRISTIAN, THE WARRIOR

I met Christian Heady at a Monster Jam event in 2020 before COVID-19 shut down the live entertainment industry. He was a normal kid who loved football and big trucks doing backflips.

A year later, Christian showed up in Tampa, Florida, to attend one of our first events after the pandemic shutdown, but he had a much different look to him. He was months into cancer treatment, and he had lost a lot of weight and most of his hair. A tumor surrounded a major artery in his neck area that could not be surgically removal. After numerous trial treatments, he ultimately passed away in September 2021.

During the final six months of Christian's life, I got to know him quite well and was always awestruck by his willingness to help others during his own battle. He was raising money for pediatric cancer organizations through awareness of his own sickness and battle. He loved shoes, the Kansas City Chiefs, and Monster Jam. He wanted to come to as many Monster Jam events as he could to support me, while all of us were actively trying to find ways to give him support. He constantly encouraged his family and friends, even when he had plenty of days where he was too tired to move. Christian was a finisher. He fought the good fight and finished the race, and I'll be forever grateful for my friend who taught me how to finish right. Difference makers are *finishers*.

You can't control what life throws at you, but you do control how you respond. The circumstances of life don't change the purpose of your life. From getting to know families battling cancer, I've learned that our typical daily problems—such as being stuck in an airport after a canceled flight or slow traffic at rush hour—aren't among the mountains standing in front of us. Those problems are pebbles in our shoes that distract us from emptying our fuel tank in our pursuit of making a real impact. When mountainous problems like cancer come into our lives, we better know how to shift into a gear we never knew we had.

What about you? There are going to be times when you are forced to empty your fuel tank while you thrash to finish a "race," but will you be up for the task? If you know where to make your pit stops, possess a "one more lap" mentality, and remain focused on finishing, you've got a fighting chance. That's what real-life thrashes require of you.

FIND YOUR GROOVE AND STAY IN IT

Following the pandemic-caused "break," I was one of six drivers (down from fifty-five before the pandemic) that Monster Jam kept onboard to run a limited event schedule. Insanely grateful that I was able to continue driving and providing for my family during such loss and uncertainty, I felt extremely guilty to consider retiring after the 2021 COVID-19 season. Monster Jam was one of the first organizations in the world to start doing live events again, and even professional football teams were using our "pod seating" model to get fans back into stadiums. Monster Jam went from eight tours before the pandemic down to a single tour for 2021, but we were fortunate to do events at all given the state of the live entertainment industry at that point.

A normal season would include one or two stadium competitions per weekend, but we did three to four stadium competitions in a single weekend that year. A few months in, I experienced quite a bit of mental fatigue after a lot of physical battering—doing so many events in such a compressed stretch of time. A Monster Jam driver's body can only take so much abuse from backflips and crashes. That battering and the longer weekend requirements that pulled me away from home more than normal made me question if I wanted to renew my contract. An extremely vivid dream convinced me to continue.

As I've already shared, my grandfather has always been my greatest influence, both while he lived and even now after his death. I still recall specific guidance he gave me to handle a particular type of situation. I can still hear his voice. What can I say? It just resurfaces and pops into my head at opportune moments.

When he was teaching me to drive a Top Fuel dragster, explaining how to keep a 300 mph vehicle stable wasn't an easy task for him. You might think dragsters just go in a straight line for a quarter mile and that's all there is to it, but that's not true. When you stand behind a 10,000-horsepower machine that accelerates faster than anything on wheels that man has made, you watch as it fights and dances all over the track throughout the entire four-second launch. The key to being a good driver is looking far enough down the track and essentially re-aiming the car as it makes a move, much like shooting an arrow from a bow.

One part of the track is called "the groove." It's a dark black section with the most rubber on it. The dragster's tires need rubber to keep traction and maximize its speed. When you go outside of the groove, you can lose both traction and control of the car, which can result in a disastrous day. Doing so has claimed many lives in the sport when an out-of-control dragster decides to fight gravity and fly through the air. My grandfather would sit down with me before each run and help me read the groove of the track, advising me how to keep the car hooked into it.

In the midst of my turmoil during the post-pandemic 2021 season, I had one of the most vivid dreams I've ever had. In it, my grandfather was younger than he was when I knew him, about forty years old. I was battling stuff both on and off the track in real life, getting my butt kicked in the process, and I felt extremely lost. In this dream, I explained the problems I was having to my grandfather, and he simply responded with, "Find the groove, and stay in it."

Life seems to toss us around on the track every day and throw us outside of the groove, where we lose our traction.

We inevitably are forced to ease off the throttle and slow down for safety, abandoning the run. When we again find the groove, we can stay on the throttle to accelerate at speeds unimaginable to the generations before us.

Difference makers *fight* to stay in the groove—our calling, our purpose. We *fight* not to abandon the run, not to give up until we hit that finish line. We relentlessly *fight* to empty the whole fuel tank so we can shake the earth and leave our mark. Somewhere out there, someone is waiting on you to finish your race. The question is, are you willing to thrash? Are you willing to empty yourself to to make the biggest impact possible?

TUNE-UP

1. When was the last time you considered your tank empty? What caused it?
2. What or who refuels you? How often should you be getting refueled?
3. What in your life is overdue for you to finish? What is your next step toward crossing the finish line?

6

ACCELERATE: 4TH GEAR

Drive with Purpose

"Radio check."

"Yep, Bryce. We hear you. Can you hear us?"

"Yep, all good on my end," I answered.

"So, what do you think? How are you feeling about this?"

I could tell my crew chief's question had a lot of nerves tied around it. I was strapped in and about to attempt a Guinness World Record for speed in a monster truck—a 12,000-pound truck with 66-inch-tall tires that each weighed 800 pounds and weren't intended for high speeds. No monster truck had ever reached 100 mph, let alone crashed at 100 mph! At that speed, the truck has the potential to vibrate itself apart and send the driver tumbling down the concrete dragstrip. Everyone involved in this attempt had good reason to be nervous.

"We got this. Let's go make some history," I said.

That day, I was strangely confident about the results. I wasn't afraid of crashing or the thousands of contingencies that could arise at any moment to prevent us from writing our names in the history books. I was just excited to step on the throttle and make history. I got the sense, though, that I might have been the only one present who was confident that we'd hit our 100-mph target.

Our practice runs the previous day hadn't gone well. We were in Florida in June, and the humidity was terrible. Since a race engine thrives on cool, dry air to make power, humidity is its enemy. That morning, the gauge that measures humidity was essentially telling us it was raining outside. Not good. We couldn't postpone to October because we were filming a special show on the Discovery Channel. It was now or never.

"Ok, Bryce. Go ahead and fire up. The track is clear," the crew chief instructed.

There's something that happens as a driver when you start a 1,500-horsepower engine. All the butterflies in your stomach are obliterated. You drop the visor on your helmet, and the atmosphere becomes "man versus machine." Total focus. You're not thinking about the mistake from the day before. You see only the track in front of you, and you're confident in the plan as you feel the vibrations coming through the steering wheel, originating from the howling motor sitting three feet behind you. I shifted the truck out of park, past neutral, and into first gear.

It was go time.

I stabbed the throttle, shifted the gears, and went hurtling down the track. The vibrations halfway down became intense. If you've ever been to the hardware store and watched the paint shaker mixing a can of paint, you can picture how my eyeballs felt in my eye sockets. At that point, I was focused on keeping my foot down on the throttle and holding the steering wheel as straight as I could until I reached the finish line.

As it rapidly approached, I executed our plan to get the truck slowed down. Dropping my foot completely off the throttle would cause such an intense shift forward of the massive machine's 12,000-pound weight that I could lose control. As I saw the finish line whiz past, I slowly decreased the throttle and brought the truck to a complete stop in about a quarter mile. Our radios didn't reach from the starting line to the end of the track where I finally stopped to shut the engine off, and the silence was deafening. The crew finally arrived in a vehicle behind me and didn't say a word.

"Well, did we break the record?" I asked.

No response. My heart sank as I assumed we had missed our 100-mph mark. We started up the truck, and they escorted me back to the other end of the track to the starting line. I pulled off my helmet, climbed down out of the truck, and asked again, "How far off were we?"

Our lead official walked over to me with a huge smile and finally broke the news. "You did it! 100.3 miles per hour! You're officially a Guinness World Record holder!" I let out a thunderous roar with every vein in my forehead popping out from the excitement. Our team had prepared for two months for that moment. We'd created a plan and adjusted along the way, and I got to be the one to launch it down the track.

The following year, I opened the 2022 Guinness World Records book and saw our Great Clips Mohawk Warrior truck with my name stamped on it. It was surreal. So many sacrifices, late nights, and risks along the way. So many failures to overcome. So many unexpected turns that required creative adjustments. Yet, as I saw my name in that book, none of the pain from the lessons I had to learn throughout my journey accompanied it. Only one thought dominated my mind at that moment. I couldn't help but think about how close I had been to never having any of this happen: just a few years ago, I was choosing a life of safety. I nearly chose to chase after a comfortable life instead of pursuing this dream—to becoming stuck in neutral instead of finding this gear that drove me to so many amazing moments like this one. It wasn't until my former life of safety and comfort blew up in my face that I was forced to shift into another gear I hadn't realized I had at the time.

⚙ ⚙ ⚙

Nothing could have prepared me for the sheer violence of accelerating from zero to 300 mph in four seconds in a Top Fuel dragster. The first pass I ever made in the car was in 2009, and I ended up with a bruise as big as a softball in the middle of my back, the result of being slammed against the seat. The experience is indescribable: going from zero to 100 mph in less than a second in 60 feet, then continuing to accelerate violently through the finish line while the impact I feel against the seat gets more intense every millisecond that the clutch applies more horsepower advancing down the track. It's like something out of a sci-fi movie—a Star Trek episode maybe.

I'll admit that the day I finished my licensing in Top Fuel, after submitting all the required passes and hitting the mandatory speeds, I held my official Top Fuel license with some of the most intense happiness and self-pride I've ever experienced. It had been my entire life's goal to get that license. The dream had created so much passion in my chest that it drove me to overcome any obstacle that came up along the way. I assumed passion would be enough to keep me running at that pace forever. I never expected a polite, seventy-five-year-old lady named Betty to slam on my brakes.

I met Betty one afternoon in 2010 when I sat next to her on a flight. After she finally got done telling me all about her grandkids, who would be waiting for her at our destination, she asked me where I was headed and why. I could not wait to tell her about all the cool stuff I was doing. Softening my voice so the hundreds of other people on the plane wouldn't get wind of my self-induced celebrity status and rush me seeking autographs, I said, "Well, Betty, I'm a professional Top Fuel driver, and I'm flying to go work for a race team this weekend." I then sat there waiting for Betty to start praising me, but she sweetly responded with, "Isn't it nice that you can get all of that out of your system at such a young age!" I don't remember my response, but I'll never forget the feeling I had at that moment. I felt betrayed.

I was working seven different jobs at that stage in my life and putting every dime I could make into my dream of making a career out of professional drag racing. I would change clothes between one job and the next while driving down the road in an old Hyundai Sonata with a bent frame that went through brand new tires every year. I was struggling, fighting, and spending every dime I worked hard for, but I saw it as a privilege. I felt like other people weren't willing to go through what I was going through at my age to make this happen. But I was secretly afraid I'd make one wrong move and screw the whole thing up. I'd secretly think to myself, "Is there a finish line to all of this?" I feared that my intense action would become my new normal forever.

Looking back, I'm thankful for Betty's response on that flight. After I drank my ginger ale and ate my pretzels, I started to dissect the feelings Betty had churned up—as if her last name was Crocker and I was a bucket of butter. It was on that airplane that, unbeknownst to her, Betty helped me decide that this wasn't just something I had to get out of my system. I decided I was built for the racing life. I was willing to do whatever it took to make it. Yes, I was passionate. But at that moment, I accepted that my purpose for being on this earth was to impact the world through motorsports.

I believe we all have a purpose, but not enough people have made the decision to accept theirs. Some people don't see their purpose clearly enough, so they live stuck in neutral or drive in a lower gear that makes them feel more comfortable for surviving the demands life throws their way. Maybe they've suffered a setback that keeps the shift knob set to the wrong gear. Recognizing when this has happened is the first step toward shifting into a higher gear to accelerate your efforts to live the life you're capable of. Without prioritizing purpose, you have instead settled for a life of convenience. How often do you make decisions based on convenience instead of your purpose?

When I realized my purpose, I started looking for inconvenient decisions to make. Looking for ways to inconvenience myself became a game. Instead of finding a reason not to make another six-hour trip to our race shop, I began looking forward to the time in the car as a chance to listen to audiobooks that coached me on developing a positive mindset. I would sit in front of a computer screen at night in my few moments of spare time, completing eye muscle exercises to improve my peripheral vision. That helped me in two ways. It enhanced my reading speed, which meant I could pore through business and self-help books more quickly; and the exercises also strengthened my eye muscles to where they could handle the violent acceleration of the Top Fuel dragster.

Instead of stopping for fast food lunches every day, I'd pack a peanut-butter-and-jelly sandwich like I was back in elementary school so I could reinvest that $10 into my dream. In fact, at one point I found a meal replacement vitamin and mineral pack that cost $2.50 per day, and I started taking it and even skipped some meals without causing my nutrition to suffer. Was I hungry? Yes. But my appetite to chase my dreams was far greater.

Those were all inconvenient sacrifices to make, but each little decision eventually added up to big results. In a time in my life when it felt almost impossible to get any traction on my dreams, proactively looking for ways to inconvenience myself became a guiding star when all else failed. Isn't it funny though, that my life started to accelerate faster than a zero to 300 mph Top Fuel dragster when I made this shift toward inconvenience? I'll admit that this sort of shift is all predicated on knowing your purpose, which can feel easier said than done. So, how do you identify your purpose?

EQUIP YOUR PASSION, FIND YOUR PURPOSE

As I sat on that airplane with Betty, I took an audit of why I was so passionate about racing. I thought about how I grew up weed eating the fence line at my grandfather's dragstrip. My passion for racing ran deep because of the late nights I spent with my family at the track and those moments of seeing the win light pop on at the end of the track when I drove our family's junior dragster. I saw the respect my grandfather had in professional drag racing, and the way the community embraced his wisdom and faith. It was undeniable that the world of motorsports needed more positive influences with leaders ready to serve others. I became passionate enough to believe that I would be one of those influences and leave my mark on this world through motorsports.

From the time I was twelve years old and first saw one go down the track, I daydreamed about driving a Top Fuel dragster. I didn't care how long it would take. If I didn't have the chance to drive one until I was sixty years old, I was still willing to go the distance. My brother came to me years ago claiming he also had a dream of driving a Top Fuel dragster. I responded with, "Great! If it took you forty years to do it, with effort every day to get there, would you still chase it?" His honest response was, "Probably not." Achieving your dreams might take longer than you realize, and feeling OK about a potentially longer timeline than you originally planned could be a solid clue that you're on the right path.

Understanding your self-imposed time limit on your goals is a big litmus test for whether your passion can develop into purpose. Your purpose shouldn't have time constraints to determine success. Purpose is much more about who you become along the way. It's good to have time frames to measure your incremental gain, but most people who claim to have a goal in life really have a two- to three-year time limit on making it happen. To me, that's just a pursuit of an idea, not a commitment to walk with purpose.

After I birthed my dream to get my Top Fuel license, I spent the next six years—between ages thirteen and nineteen—as a crew guy learning every inch of how these 10,000-horsepower machines made it down the track. The physics behind applying that much power from a standstill is ridiculous. Essentially, you need only to apply part of the 10,000-horsepower at the initial launch, and slowly (from zero to two seconds) apply all the horsepower as the car accelerates; otherwise you'd never get the dragster to keep traction for the full length of the racetrack. I was devoted to working on motors, learning how to tune the clutch, and getting my mind ready to eventually be in the driver's seat.

I was equipping my passion with knowledge—all so I could chase my purpose: to utilize motorsports to influence other people. When I finally got my chance at age twenty to drive and get my license, my learning curve was shockingly short. I knew the start-up procedures like the back of my hand because I'd run through them in my mind thousands of times (and even given a speech about them to my public-speaking class during my freshman year of high school).

Look at it this way: passion is like an engine with a lifespan. No engine can run forever. You can have the best engine with the most power just sitting on a stand in the shop completely useless. It isn't until you install that engine into a race car and take it out to compete at the track that it finds a purpose. Like the engine, you can sit useless on the couch idling in your passion, revving it up every now and then. Or you can give your passion a vehicle with which to accelerate toward accomplishing incredible things. That's what equipping your passion to find your purpose looks like. You just have to find the right vehicle—or means—with which to do it.

FINDING MEANING

Admittedly, finding a vehicle for your passions sounds great, doesn't it? But while we're in the process of equipping our passions to get there, it can be such a difficult grind. While I was in the midst of my seven-job stint, I remember one night where I felt incredibly sorry for myself. Late one evening, I walked outside of an office building after getting rejected for a sponsorship. I could hear people laughing and cheering from a property, my view of them blocked by many trees between us. What I could see were the softball field lights igniting the sky above the trees and narrowly gleaming through a few branches. Whoever was playing in that softball league was having more fun than I had experienced in months.

I stood there for about ten minutes just listening to the crack of the bat against the ball, teammates clapping for one another, and the gasps from everyone as a baserunner approached home plate, the crowd wondering if they would score or not. It was clear that whichever team was trying to score was passionate about winning that softball game. At that moment I thought, "Am I ever going to have any fun again?"

Sure, I was pursuing some amazing stuff and occasionally driving a Top Fuel dragster. I was traveling the country. But I was exhausted and without any hope that my efforts would turn into long-term results. As I got into my car that night, I was searching for meaning to this struggle. "Why does achieving my dream have to be *this* hard?" I thought. "Is this all even worth it?" If I was equipping my passion, I needed to find meaning in it to keep going long enough to turn it into purpose. Thankfully, I was given the perfect book to help me do that.

A few days later, I sat down with a mentor to express my frustration and ask for guidance. He handed me a book titled

Man's Search for Meaning. The author, Viktor Frankl, outlines how he survived the Holocaust when others perished. Pretty good qualifications for writing such a book, don't you think? Frankl suggests that finding the meaning of our lives isn't some mental awakening that happens randomly. He discusses three ways to identify our meaning in life:

1. *Creating a work or accomplishing a deed.* Think through what you've accomplished so far and identify unique skill sets or passions you possess that enabled you to get it done. These breadcrumbs might lead you onto a clearer path than you previously thought was available.
2. *Experiencing something or encountering someone.* Have you visited a region or country on a trip and felt a strong pull to serve that community or culture? It could be as close as your next-door neighbor or on the opposite side of the world, but when have you felt a natural draw to help?
3. *The attitude we take toward unavoidable suffering.* "In some way, suffering ceases to be suffering at the moment it finds a meaning, such as the meaning of sacrifice." Turning your tragedy into triumph is "uniquely human," as Frankl reveals. As an example, I know too many parents who have had to watch their child go through pediatric cancer and then

> become advocates to raise awareness and support for other families going through the same situation. They've chosen to find purpose and meaning after their devastation, to create beauty from ashes.

Frankl writes about how too many people are trying to solve some abstract meaning of life when they should be looking at their real-life situations and relationships to learn how to make their next move and decision based on what they've experienced, learned, or loved so far. My experience from listening to the sounds of the softball game through the trees made me realize I was uniquely skilled and passionate about using motorsports to impact the world. I also found meaning when I thought about how unique it was that I had experienced the thrill of driving a Top Fuel dragster. And lastly, I found meaning in the attitude I normally took toward my suffering while trying to make my crazy dream come to fruition.

My attitude stank the night I listened to the softball game. Most of the time, though, thankfully, my attitude has been focused on the opportunity to grow and learn to be more effective in pursuing my long-term purpose. Each time I have overcome an obstacle, I've felt like I was adding a tool to my life's tool belt that would be utilized in my future. I began to grow unshakeable confidence that my purpose could propel me to a bigger and better future, regardless of the inconveniences that knocked me off track along the way.

It's important to move toward successfully operating in your purpose because it keeps you grounded when circumstances change. What would happen if you were to meet the love of your life next week at a coffee shop? You previously found meaning in your career, but your circumstances suddenly changed that Thursday when a stranger near you ordered a peppermint-white-chocolate mocha, then turned to you to say, "It's like Christmas in a cup!" Forget about your career for a moment and get that girl's number! Your circumstances change when you get a call from your mom that she has stage 4 lung cancer. Your meaning in life had been about traveling the world until you began to grapple with the thought that your days with your mom are numbered. Now you find meaning in your life by simply spending time with her.

Passions can change. The meaning of your life can change as you experience new things. But a real overall purpose will remain intact regardless of what is thrown at you. That's why battling through the "equipping" phase is so critical. Equipping your passion is rarely convenient. If you can find meaning in your struggle, you will have enough patience to get through the arduous stage of equipping your passions to find your purpose. Situations might change, but purpose is the steady foundation to making a real impact.

PURPOSED SHIFT

My résumé starts with years of drag racing, then lists several years working at a soccer organization, then switches to corporate recruiting, and then jumps over to monster trucks. Yup, it appears odd, like I'm all over the map. If you didn't know any better, seeing this might cause you to assume I either failed, got bored, or operated in a completely reactive mindset by accepting whatever came my way. As if I were some fickle, rudderless guy. Although I have admitted failure in my drag racing pursuits, that doesn't answer the question of why I didn't get back into drag racing right away.

After a few years away from that sport, my passion for it hadn't changed. I still love drag racing. But when I had the opportunity to get into Monster Jam, it wasn't a question about whether I was passionate about driving monster trucks; I wasn't. I didn't feel one way or the other. Keep in mind, I had never been to a Monster Jam event before I started talking to the company. If I were making the decision based only on my passion and not my purpose, I would've turned down the opportunity to test drive a Monster Jam truck.

When that door opened, however, I filtered the chance through my *purpose* instead of just my *passion*. When they called me back a few months after my first driving test to ask me to drive on a tour the following season, I again filtered the decision through my purpose. If I believed I was meant to change people's lives through motorsports, wouldn't this align with that purpose? When Betty shook me up on that airplane years prior, did I determine I was only meant to influence people through drag racing? No. I never would've guessed as a kid that monster trucks were going to be such a massive part of my racing career, but they have kept me operating in my purpose.

Today, I'm just as fervent about driving a Monster Jam truck as I was driving a Top Fuel car. In fact, I'd imagine my passion is greater. For 120 days out of the year, I'm living an insanely cool life with Monster Jam. I get on an airplane and fly to a city across America where my truck is ready and waiting for me when I arrive. I spend Friday speaking to media outlets promoting the event and my brand, and then have some track practice. On Saturday I spend three-and-a-half hours signing autographs and taking pictures with fans before climbing up in my truck for the event later that evening, where I jump 30 feet in the air and backflip a 12,000-pound machine in front of 50,000 screaming fans.

The best part is that we have amazing Monster Jam crew members who fix the truck when I tear it up and have it ready for the next weekend. I wake up the next morning and fly home to see my family for a few days before I leave to do it all again. What's not to love about that?

Yes, I'm passionate about getting to do all of that. But my purpose is to impact the Monster Jam community. My purpose is to make every single fan that comes through my autograph line during that three-and-a-half hour "pit party" feel like the most important person I've met all day. And while competing, my purpose is to inspire the next generation to believe they have what it takes to chase their own dreams, even if they don't involve motorsports.

If I could help one person each weekend learn to equip their passion to ultimately find their purpose, I'd take that as a life well-lived! That's what gets my engine revving. That's what pushes me to accelerate at a back-breaking speed to maximize every opportunity that comes my way. I'm thankful I've been able to equip my passion through the years to live my purpose and establish my platform, one Grandpa would endorse and be proud of.

I sincerely believe that purpose is not as difficult to identify as we've made it. If you're passionate about something and willing to inconvenience yourself enough to equip that passion, you'll find your purpose. Making decisions based on your purpose and not what is convenient at the time will propel you to achieve speeds in life you never knew were possible. All it takes is some courage to stab that throttle pedal and uncover your purpose. I'll warn you of one thing, however: the faster you accelerate, the more prepared you have to be to overcome resistance along the way. Becoming the best version of yourself will require a shift to being willing to fight through some obstacles, and that's the exact direction we're going next!

TUNE-UP

1. Who are one or two people in your life you would describe as "passionate"? What attributes do they possess that make them so?
2. If you could be paid $1 million a year to do anything, what would it be?
3. How would the world, your community, or your family change once you equip your passion and operate in it every day?

7

ROADBLOCKS: 5TH GEAR

Prepare for Resistance

One of my first nights around other Monster Jam drivers almost ended in a fight. This was during a training summit in Florida to prepare for the upcoming 2016 season, and all the drivers were there. I was brand-new to the sport. The only person I knew was one of the Grave Digger drivers, Morgan Kane, who had introduced me to Monster Jam. I had hosted Morgan on his soccer recruiting trip to Campbell University a few years earlier, and we had stayed friends while we both pursued our separate motorsports dreams.

When I got out of professional drag racing, Morgan had been the person who convinced me to someday consider breaking into the monster truck industry. He connected me with Monster Jam right away, but it took the company four more years to call me back with an opportunity to test drive a Monster Jam truck. It's crazy that this whole chapter of my life with Monster Jam started from hosting some kid in college.

Looking back on that night in Florida at the training weekend, I laugh at how Morgan tried subtly to warn me—with raised eyebrows—as I headed out of the hotel lobby to walk to dinner with a group of veteran drivers who, in hindsight, weren't very open-minded to rookie drivers.

Since my whole world was drag racing and I hadn't grown up around monster trucks, I didn't know who any of the other drivers were. I wasn't just a rookie; I was an outsider. I had never even been to a Monster Jam event until I started talking with the company about driving.

One of the Monster Jam executives recommended I walk over and pick the brain of a guy who had a massively successful career in professional dirt bike racing and had made the shift over to Monster Jam. His name was Damon Bradshaw. Damon was extremely kind to me as we stood in a banquet hall following a training session, and he patiently answered multiple questions from me about his experience with the career move. It was such a positive conversation for both of us that he invited me to walk over to a restaurant with him and some other veteran drivers to keep the conversation going. Big mistake on my part.

I agreed to go to dinner for two reasons: to keep chatting with Damon and to take the opportunity to meet another driver named Cam McQueen, who was scheduled to be my tourmate for the upcoming 2016 season. Once we got to the restaurant, Damon introduced me to the other drivers. Everyone was nice and shook my hand . . . except one.

"Bryce, this is Lee O'Donnell," Damon said.

I looked at Lee, extended my hand, and said, "Hey, Lee. I'm Bryce Kenny. Nice to meet you."

"You're a first-year driver?" Lee asked.

"Yea, I'll actually be on tour with Cam next year," I said.

Lee looked me in the eyes, left his hand by his side, and said, "Don't f----ing talk to me until after your second year." Then he walked away as a few other drivers looked at me with amusement to see how I'd react.

I was embarrassed, but I was also really ticked off. And remember, I had no idea who this guy was. He had no idea who I was either. I tried to shake it off as we walked to our table. Then, as we all started to sit down, Lee and I somehow managed to sit right across from one another. It happened when I grabbed the seat next to Damon so we could continue our conversation. Lee started laughing and said, "I don't sit with rookies. Go sit on the other end of the table!" Now, I'm as stubborn as a mule; I wouldn't budge. I even gave a courtesy laugh to ease the tension. He laughed again and said, "This new guy thinks I'm kidding!"

I ignored him, and he kept pressing me for another fifteen minutes. Once I realized this was going to become a scene and take away from the environment, I said to him, "Are you kidding me? You're being serious right now with this? I don't even know who you are. But I'm not going to waste my time with you either." Lee laughed some more. I finally got up and walked away to avoid things getting physical. I sat near Cam to get to know him as I had originally intended.

Just when I thought this new Monster Jam chapter of life was starting to gear up, I got blindsided by someone who made me start questioning if this culture was something I wanted to commit to. Whatever balloon I was holding seemed to be deflating quickly. It taught me, though, that resistance will always show up once we make a shift into that next gear in our lives.

Growing up, my mom used a football analogy to prepare my brothers and me for these types of altercations by saying, "Just remember when you're the one running the ball down the field, there will always be someone out there wanting to knock it out of your hands." That is what this gear is all about: being prepared for resistance when it inevitably comes. Being ready either to avoid or break through roadblocks requires skill, tenacity, and sometimes just good old-fashioned stubbornness.

MONSTROUS CAREER SHIFT

That first year driving a Monster Jam truck in 2016, I felt like a fish out of water. My whole life had been drag racing up until that point, and I had given up my Top Fuel driving career five years before. Looking back, though, that five-year gap was monumental in setting a foundation for me to pursue this Monster Jam chapter. I got married during that five-year hiatus as well. McKenzie and I bought a house, and then we started a family. Around that time, I also started my new career in executive recruiting. I'm very thankful for that time to "get my house in order," but the decision to leave my safe and secure corporate job to get back into motorsports was one the hardest decisions of my life.

The executive search firm I worked for was Charles Aris, and I focused my efforts there mostly on placing CFOs and CEOs into private equity–backed companies. And I loved it! I got to talk to executives every single day and hear about what different companies were doing out in the market. I describe the experience as getting a real-world master's in business administration. I remember having a reference call with the CEO of a major publicly traded company and looking up his salary while we were on the call just for fun. When I saw his multi-million-dollar base salary, I nearly spit out my coffee.

I had great conversations with the "movers and shakers" of corporate America everyday! And I became really good at it. My career was budding and brought with it a healthy income. I was beginning to build out my own practice and discovered I had the potential to more than double my income with the search firm when I got the call from Monster Jam. I was torn. To make the shift away from my corporate career and into Monster Jam meant leaving my safety net behind. I also hadn't grown up around the monster truck community. Sometimes a good opportunity can keep us from a great opportunity, and I struggled to figure out which of those buckets Monster Jam fit into.

I knew I'd be back in motorsports eventually. I just thought I'd take the route my grandfather had taken by making enough money to fund everything myself. I wasn't afraid of taking forty years to get involved again if that was what it required of me. So was I tied to getting back into drag racing, or could Monster Jam be the opportunity I had always dreamed of?

The offer to leave my corporate job to pursue Monster Jam brought several mental obstacles for me to deal with. Leaving would require me to take a 30 percent pay cut. My executive recruiting job required about 60-70 hours a week, six days a week, and about 300 days a year. But that job didn't require more than a 20-minute commute. With Monster Jam, I'd be traveling about 120 days a year away from my family and living out of a suitcase. I would be giving up my safety net of a longer-term career trajectory because, like professional athletes in other sports such as football and baseball, a Monster Jam driver's driving days are numbered. And I would be trading it all in for a much riskier driving contract that had no promises beyond the term limits we agreed on. I tried to break through these mental obstacles for months.

The day I made the decision to leave my safe corporate life for a riskier one, I was standing in my garage talking on the phone. As I paced around the garage talking to a business colleague, my eyes started catching the items I'd hung on the wall. Pictures of the different race teams I've been with. Banners. A time slip from my first Top Fuel race pass. A massive construction-style sign that my family used for racing promotions that read "Speed Limit Not to Exceed 300 mph." A picture of my grandfather's first four-second Top Fuel pass, which commemorated what had been a monumental moment for our family to have him join the exclusive four-second club. I had memories all over the place linked to motorsports. What wasn't on the wall? A picture of some CEO I'd placed or any other corporate achievement.

I was built for motorsports. I had my answer. I got off the call I was on and immediately called Monster Jam to tell them I was ready to go. Since then, Monster Jam has become my second family, and I'm grateful I had the courage to head for the unknown. Looking back, those mental obstacles weren't nearly as big and scary as they seemed at the moment of my indecision. They just required me to shift into my next gear and see the path around them. Sometimes your hesitation causes the roadblocks in life to appear much bigger than they are. If you're not careful, you accept a status as an underdog longer than you should.

UNDERDOGS

Imagine if NASCAR owned everything: the teams, the cars, the crews, the drivers. That's how Monster Jam operates. When they initially called me to train in one of their trucks, I had an attitude of, "Well, it'll at least be a cool story to tell my kids one day!" I honestly had no idea what I was getting myself into.

The first truck I drove was called "Monster Mutt," a dog-themed Monster Jam truck that welcomed a lot of "Mutt Cutts" memes affectionately sent to me by my wife (like the dog-themed van in the movie *Dumb and Dumber*). My truck had big floppy ears that bounced around when I launched it 20 feet in the air. I felt pretty silly driving it, but young fans loved it. I was having fun, even if I wasn't driving one of the more iconic brands in the sport like Grave Digger. Everyone knows that name!

The first time I lined up to compete against Grave Digger, I felt like a major underdog. If I was David, he was Goliath. And yes, he kicked my butt that first race. I had just gotten the chance to drive a sponsored truck when Great Clips came on board and sponsored a truck called "Mohawk Warrior." The Grave Digger driver in the other lane was Adam Anderson, son of Dennis Anderson. Adam and I have become good friends over the years. We also hate to lose to each other, as we often discuss on the monster truck–themed podcast we co-host called *Gears and Nachos*. Our rivalry's win-loss record is still tilted in his favor as of this writing, much to my dismay. At one point, I had eight crashes in racing in my entire career, and every single one of those crashes was against Adam. When I see that "black-and-green wrecking machine" in the other lane, I find this intense focus that is reserved only for trying to beat him.

Early in my monster truck–driving career, I didn't feel pressure to win against more experienced drivers. As the underdog, I concentrated on learning to compete in an unfamiliar sport. I lost. A lot. I also learned. A lot. I learned how to win and represent a brand. But being the underdog can feel isolating too. We develop this "second string" mentality if we aren't careful.

Growing up, I started on every sports team I was part of. I never sat on the bench until I got to college to play NCAA Division 1 soccer. There, I developed a mentality that I wasn't first-string caliber and unknowingly accepted this second-string mentality. When we think we're less than others, everything (and everyone) appears to be an obstacle. It's OK to be the underdog, but seeing our best version of ourselves allows us to get off the bench and into the game of life as a first-string-caliber athlete. The lessons we learn with a first-string mentality are far greater because we're "on the field" playing the game. We can only learn so much from sitting on the bench waiting for our turn. The key to making this mental shift is knowing there is no coach waiting to call your number. In life, *we* get to decide when we go from being second string to first string by no longer accepting our current situation.

BECOME A MONSTER

We never hear the word *meek* anymore. For most, meekness seems to translate to weakness. But having meekness means you're able to fight yet choose to be peaceful. It means incredible strength under control. Psychologist and media commentator Jordan Peterson was a guest on Joe Rogan's podcast one time, and he talked about how society is causing people to be afraid to be tough, strong, and able to really battle.

He said the world is trying to paint those people as monsters. I like what Peterson goes on to say, though. He says, "You should be a monster. Everyone says you should be harmless, virtuous. That you should sheath your competitive instinct. That you shouldn't try to win. That you don't want to be too aggressive or too assertive. That you want to take a back seat and all of that. No, that's wrong. You should be a monster, an absolute monster, and then you should learn how to control it."

Growing up, I always felt that authority figures in my life kept trying to pull the reins back on my intensity. I felt like a monster in the eyes of others. Incredible strength kept under control isn't easy to build.

Most people are stronger than they realize, simply from getting their teeth kicked in by life. It's the "under control" part that seems to elude most of us. Learning to control the warrior side of us—the side that's focused, tough, and unapologetic for our core beliefs—comes from constant effort and discipline in personal growth. It also comes from having proper mentorship, which we will discuss more in the next chapter.

I had to learn that the world of racing existed a certain way before I stepped into it with my own desires and aspirations. It wouldn't just accept me with open arms once I walked through the door with a dream in hand. The racing industry operated, for better or worse, in its own way, built over the years by other men and women with their own agendas. If I was going to pursue a racing career, I had to learn how to influence situations to maximize every opportunity and connection that came to me.

What I needed to learn was *leadership*. John C. Maxwell, arguably one of the top leadership experts in the world, says in his book *The 21 Irrefutable Laws of Leadership*, "The accurate measure of leadership is influence—nothing more, nothing less." My solution to learning how to influence people was books. I dove headfirst into reading books that advocated a positive mindset (Napoleon Hill, *Think and Grow Rich*, and David J. Schwartz, *The Magic of Thinking Big*), people skills (Dale Carnegie, *How to Win Friends and Influence People*), and encouraged me to take more risks and have more faith (Erwin Raphael McManus, *The Barbarian Way*, and John Eldredge, *Walking with God*).

I used to hate reading, but I hated being an idiot more. I've become addicted to the personal growth that reading such books produces in me. Books have given me the edge I've needed over the years to manage sponsors in corporate boardrooms, creatively engage with my fan base, and even negotiate my personal contracts. Books have been my solution to controlling the monster inside. They have allowed me to become a more effective leader to influence people, situations, and outcomes for the better.

Your solution could be books, podcasts, conferences, church, or a strong mentorship—or, like most of us, a combination of these things. Whatever enables you to build incredible strength under control. It takes effort to consistently submit the worst versions of ourselves to the potential of our best versions. That's what we're really doing, isn't it? Allowing our worst versions to dissipate so a better version can emerge?

Being willing to equip ourselves with the tools, the mindset, and the work ethic to break through our roadblocks requires us to stop apologizing for our desire to fight and beckons us to sharpen our swords to prepare for the resistance when it shows up at our door. I didn't know what real peace was until I equipped myself to defend it at all costs. Like the Chinese proverb paraphrases, "It's better to be a warrior in a garden than a gardener in a war."

THE FIRST ROADBLOCK

When I look back honestly at my moments of feeling lost along the journey to become a professional driver, I realize how I have often let mental roadblocks take away my peace. Sometimes life is so difficult that it forces us to live in a reactive state. We wonder why we can't seem to catch a break. When I made the decision to leave my safe corporate career for Monster Jam, it wasn't a reactive decision. It was a purposeful attack against the life of monotony I had previously built and a move to get back into living my purpose. I couldn't see all the steps I would need to take to make my career work as a professional Monster Jam driver. I could only see that first proactive decision. Had I known about all the opposition I would face in this season as a professional driver, I sometimes wonder if I would've had enough courage to start the journey. Maybe we aren't supposed to see how our whole story will unfold for that very reason.

When you break through one roadblock at a time with all your effort and strength instead of trying to overcome two at once, you typically find the resolve to break it down. The hardest roadblock to overcome is your first one. Roadblocks become easier to overcome once you know what causes them to break down, but the first step in overcoming them is your own *decision* that you're willing and able to attack them.

You're not alone. Every person with a heartbeat is secretly wondering if they have what it takes to break through their roadblocks. That's why so many people never even step on the battlefield to. Sometimes you might question whether you'll be victorious, but the only way to know the answer is to stand toe to toe with it. Regrets are reserved for inactive people as well as those who are reactive. Today, it's time for you to reject indecisiveness and fear. It's time to look in the mirror with a composed intensity that no roadblock can extinguish. You'll be shocked at what you will be able to defeat.

If you approached each roadblock with half the criticism you speak to yourself in your mind, that roadblock would crumble before you even had to make a move. It's selfish to be self-critical to the point of stagnation. When you open your mouth against your addiction, your sickness, your trauma, or whatever roadblock stands in front of you, your feet become firmly planted with conviction, direction, and clarity.

FINDING THE COURAGE

Two good endings came from my initial run-in with Lee O'Donnell. First, Lee and I eventually became buddies. Admittedly, it took a few years for me to even look at him, and I'm proud to say our only time lining up against each other in racing led to me winning. Oh yeah, I'm 1-0 against Lee forever. I haven't asked him since he retired in 2018 what he hopes his legacy is in the industry off the track, but he did leave a legacy on the track with the first-ever front flip in a Monster Jam truck. That was back in 2018 at the Monster Jam World Finals. It was a groundbreaking and ground–shaking moment that has gone viral online multiple times over the years.

I also had a polar-opposite experience from the run-in with Lee that same weekend in Florida. Dennis Anderson, the founder and pioneer of Grave Digger, saw me ordering food in a restaurant on our last night and recognized me as one of the "new guys." He didn't know my name and simply yelled, "Hey, you!" After I looked over at him with a quizzical expression, not believing he had any idea who I was, he told me to come sit with him. Given my experience with the other veteran drivers a few nights prior, I'll admit that my first thought was, "Oh great, here we go again."

This time, though, I was being welcomed with open arms by the biggest name in the sport. I had the opportunity to sit and talk with the guy in the monster truck industry who, in my opinion, built its very backbone. Our conversation that night set me up for success in this industry more than any other discussion I've had since. Hearing him talk about starting Grave Digger, his trials through the years, and how he approaches the business side of motorsports was monumental for me. It gave me the conviction I needed to commit to my racing ambitions through this avenue of Monster Jam for the long haul.

Conviction is powerful. It is the fuel you need to drive through any obstacles in your path. Roadblocks hate conviction. If you let roadblocks break your heart first, you might hesitate just long enough for them to intimidate you. If a roadblock can cause you to battle yourself first, you'll be so tired that you'll lose the energy or the courage to overcome it. That's why you have to be prepared to fight for what you want most when the resistance comes and learn to bust through the roadblocks fueled by your convictions. That's where the best version of you will emerge. And that's what incredible strength under control looks like. Are you ready for the breakthrough?

TUNE-UP

1. Who or what would you describe as "resistance" in your life? Explain.
2. If you had to rate your ability to influence a situation in your life on a scale of 1–10, what score would you give yourself? What number do you want to be? Briefly describe what type of 90-day personal growth plan you should commit to in order to get there.
3. What roadblocks in your life do you need to break through right now?

8

TROPHIES: 6TH GEAR

Feed Memories, Not Egos

I was on cloud nine the day I prepared to finish up my Top Fuel license. I was in Indianapolis at Lucas Oil Raceway, and I was scheduled to make two separate quarter-mile passes to finish my licensing requirements. Doing so and holding that license in my hands would be the ultimate trophy in my life.

That track is the capital of drag racing; it's where the US nationals event takes place each year—the most prestigious race in the sport. I had waited my whole life for that moment. I woke up and grabbed coffee, then put on black slacks, a white embroidered polo shirt, and a black leather belt with a gold buckle. On a normal race day, I'd have worn black work pants and a black T-shirt, because working on Top Fuel dragsters can get extremely dirty.

As I look back on my outfit that day, the gold buckle makes me feel the silliest for some reason. I was trying to look a certain way that day as the "hot shot" driver.

When I dreamed of becoming a professional driver, I also envisioned walking into rooms of people and them saying to each other, "That's the coolest guy I've ever seen!" My ego was so wrapped up in the pursuit of becoming a professional driver that I wouldn't just daydream about driving. I would daydream about the way I'd live my life as a professional driver as well: what my friends would think, how hot my wife would be, how strangers would describe me to others. My narcissism was off the charts. No wonder I wore a gold belt buckle the day of my final licensing runs.

The day ended up with massive complications, and even though I finished my runs, I basically lost my mind. I was thrown multiple curveballs from the track operators, wasted $5,000 of my own money (roughly the cost of a single pass in Top Fuel at the time) on a single botched run that wasn't our team's fault, and I got in the worst argument I'd ever had with my Uncle Mike (my crew chief) as a result. I shut down mentally. Mike even kicked me out of the pit area in his own frustration, after which I went and sat on the asphalt in the staging lanes at the track. I wasn't feeling sorry for myself. I was angry. I had dreamed about this day, worked tirelessly toward it for years, and the moment was absolutely nothing like I'd imagined.

My grandfather's internal mentorship was profound, but this might have been his finest moment. He quietly listened to me whine about how unfair the whole experience was. Then he said something that has always motivated me to try to keep my ego in check. He said, "You know, Bryce, one day none of us will get to do this stuff anymore. All we'll have left are the memories made along the way. We better make them good ones."

After about twenty minutes of self-reflection, I shook off the embarrassment and decided I'd do everything possible to avoid feeding my ego like that as a professional driver. I committed to prioritizing making memories with my family, teammates, and fans over making my name brighter. I shifted what type of trophies I wanted to acquire.

As a kid, I wanted to stockpile trophies. Being one of four boys in my family, we competed to see who could earn more of them. The bigger and shinier, the better! No exaggeration: I bet I had fifty trophies in my room. I have no idea where they are now that I'm an adult. Probably in a landfill.

The trophies I now cherish are small relics that take my mind to favorite memories. The American flag–themed hard hat hanging in my garage reminds me of my grandfather's

"Under Construction"-themed dragster that started this crazy journey for me. The time slip on my wall from my first full pass in a Top Fuel dragster immediately brings back the ecstatic moment I shared with my family when I got to realize that dream. The Great Clips flag that rode on the back of my Mohawk Warrior truck at my first Monster Jam World Finals in 2017 is draped in my shop; it has dirt stains on it that force me to think of the giant bear hug I gave my crew chief after we showed the world we deserved to compete on the sport's biggest stage.

These sentimental items take my mind to the finest trophies I possess: memories that will never rust or be destroyed. Having the right people in our lives will always make us better, and now I'm deeply motivated to accumulate as many of these fine trophies as possible, highlighting the many significant "people moments" in my life instead of whatever ego-feeding achievements I might have made at other people's expense.

PEOPLE OVER PROJECTS

I adamantly believe that people skills should be a class every student must take before graduating high school. Learning how to build the right group of people around us can make the difference between success and failure. When you hear the term *people skills*, you might think it's code for manipulating others to get what we want. That is so far away from what real people skills are all about.

Once I understood and believed that everyone is wired differently, it helped me understand why some people make certain decisions, why they either engage or withdraw from public environments, and how a person can love to wear yellow-highlighter sweatshirts. If our environment, the company we keep, shapes our mindset and our lives more than anything else, becoming skilled in dealing with others allows us to protect it. Since we can't all stand in a circle holding hands around a bonfire all day, we're going to end up interacting with other people.

If you're built with purpose and you're chasing dreams, other people will be part of your story; it just happens. Learning what makes each of us think, act, and respond the way we do based on our personalities and personal history enables greater opportunities to influence others for the better based on *their* needs instead of *our* wants. At the same time, we have things to accomplish, don't we? So how do we balance accomplishment with relationships with those we encounter along the way? My answer came from getting it dangerously wrong a few years back.

In 2005, I played on an extremely competitive high school soccer team. We had lost in the state championship the year prior when I was a junior, and I was extremely committed to getting a shot at redemption my senior season. We had a team principle based on Matthew 18 in the Bible that we used as a guide to confront one another in the right way when someone wronged us. It promoted a healthy team environment instead of allowing resentment to grow over time from unresolved issues. I had a few instances of having to confront a teammate or be confronted by one, since my passion could create friction with others at times. I loved to win, but I hated to think that someone out there wanted to win more than me.

Our 2005 team was working through a few preseason speed bumps that always seemed to accompany a fresh season. We got pummeled in a tournament by the same team that had beaten us in the state championship the year before. At one point, I got ticked off at a teammate who kept blabbering about why we had lost, as if he had been more committed to winning that game than I was. I thought, "This guy didn't even play a single minute of that game!" After ten minutes of being patient, I finally lost it. I verbally cut him down so hard that I made him cry. I took all my insecurities and failures on the field and funneled them into that teammate at that moment, and it shames me to write about it now, almost twenty years later.

Later that night, we were on our way back from a team dinner. As the bus stopped at the hotel, our coach stood up to address the incident since the entire team knew about how "big bully Bryce" yelled at our sweet freshman teammate. We had that Matthew 18 principle in our team agreement, and it was our coach's opportunity to drive the principle home. He said, "Guys, if you have something you need to approach someone about from this season, do not get off this bus until it's resolved."

I had already made amends with my freshman teammate, but I knew there might be a player or two whose feathers I had ruffled during the past few weeks. Immediately, and I am not exaggerating, a line began to form in the aisle of that bus with teammates who wanted to confront me about how I had wronged all of them in some way. We were only a few weeks into our season! I bet there were ten players waiting to confront me. That was the moment I realized I was too focused on the wrong trophy and needed to have more consideration for relationships along the way. I had been on a mission to win and allowed a nasty habit to creep in where I focused on my goal to win a championship trophy over my relationships with my teammates. Something had to change.

A COMMON GOAL

As I sat on that bus after dealing with all the confrontations standing in front of me, I processed my reasoning for wanting to push myself and the team so hard. Bottom line, I wanted to win a state championship. I wanted that trophy at the end of the season. At that moment though, I thought, "How miserable would it be to get to the podium to accept the trophy, and nobody is there to raise it in the air in celebration with me? Was I just using people to get where I wanted to go?"

As a seventeen-year-old kid, I had assumed nobody would care about my level of kindness (or lack of it) if we all won those championship rings in the end. The problem was that the end didn't justify the means. I had to find a way to become valuable to my teammates beyond playing hard and helping us to win. I had to care about what they wanted out of the season. That's what a great team is all about, whether it's on an athletic field, in a classroom, or in an office building. I don't care if it's soccer, debate team, a company, or Monster Jam. Any team with that works together as a unit becomes a force to be reckoned with.

After we worked through the problems and handled the confrontations in a productive manner that night on the bus, we were freed to commit together to a common goal. We decided that winning a state championship would give our program the ability to attract players who would benefit from the mentorship of our head coach and ultimately create positive ripple effects in our community. The hard work, dedication, and results started to flow until we did, in fact, hoist that championship trophy at the end of the season—together!

That 2005 season set off a pattern of success where multiple championships and even a national number-one ranking would follow in the coming seasons. Success breeds success when everyone checks their egos at the door and decides they can accomplish more together than as individual players.

FINDING URGENCY

One of my all-time favorite speakers is Zig Ziglar, who once said, "You can have everything in life you want if you will just help enough other people get what they want." When you stop chasing what your ego wants and turn your eyes to other people, your entire perspective shifts. That's when you become intentional with people and become the positive environment that will help shape their ambitions too.

Not every person in your life stays in it forever, and that's OK. Many of us initially put unrealistic expectations on ourselves, thinking that anyone we allow into our lives will be with us until we die. However, we eventually realize how foolish this is by the time we hit our twenties and our friend group changes. Not wanting to be vulnerable with others is really a desire for self-preservation, since they could eventually exit our environment. Whether someone comes into your life for a specific purpose, a period of time, or as a permanent figure, you have to recognize your own opportunity to add something valuable to their life, regardless of the time you're given.

As a result, the urgency you find in seeing the needs of others will come when you finally accept that not everyone will be a "permanent" person for you. What if today was the last chance you had to meet that need for a neighbor, and you are their best solution? That mental shift will get you off the couch and into action quicker than any excuse you can come up with. When someone turns out to be a temporary person in your life, you should start finding gratitude that you were able to make memories with them while you could instead of allowing resentment to grow because they turned out not to be a "permanent" person as you had hoped. As life changes, relationships change. That should make you constantly want to shift into this critical gear of making memories and not egos with everyone in your life. You never know which memory will be your last.

One of the most important relationships you can create is with the type of person I've referenced numerous times throughout this book. It's a relationship that has the potential to shape your environment more than anyone and help you shift into your full potential: a mentor.

FINDING A MENTOR

I'm about to ruin your night's sleep with a particular question I wrestle with that has kept me awake more than any other. We're all guilty of lying in bed after a tough day and thinking through the situations and people we experienced, unable to doze off. We think about how the things we said or did could cost us that next raise, the test grade we've been studying for, or maybe a relationship. But have you ever stopped to think about the cost of what you don't know?

For instance, if it's possible to make a million dollars a year and a person is making $45,000 a year, then not knowing how to make a million dollars a year is costing that person $955,000 every year. I'm just using an arbitrary financial goal to make my point. It is the things we don't yet know that cost us the most. If you asked me the value of mentorship, I'd draw out this financial example on a page and put a big, highlighted circle around $955,000. I'd say, "A good mentor lessens your cost of what you don't know by teaching you what you need to learn and showing you how to apply it." Realizing the cost of unlearned knowledge should stimulate humility that will open you up to finding a mentor. But don't take that sleeping aid quite yet. Hang on; this next part is critical.

We have limitless access to information on the internet, but information without application is useless. Proper mentorship is about taking the information we learn and applying it to our lives in the most efficient way possible. I've avoided more of life's land mines, whether in my marriage, as a dad, and even as a professional driver, by leveraging the knowledge and advice of other people who knew where the land mines would be along my journey. However, the value of a mentor isn't about having someone to give me the answers to life's tests. The most valuable part of having a mentor is being accountable to someone who knows me and my goals and helps shine a light on a pathway they've taken themselves. When we become accountable to people we trust, we greatly reduce our egos and set ourselves up to be more open to the things we do not know that cost us the most.

Let's look at it this way. I earned an all-expenses-paid trip in 2016 to Costa Rica after hitting all my performance targets at the executive recruiting firm. There was a nice lady named Sue whom our firm paid to come by the office to set up the trip for all the qualifiers. She familiarized us with the trip by showing us our itinerary, maps of the area, pictures of the resort, and even brochures of the different excursions we could take when we arrived.

Sue taught us a lot about Costa Rica, but she had never been there herself. When we landed, we were greeted by a guy named Mark. Mark had grown up in Costa Rica and knew of all the fun to be had there. We asked him about the best swimming hole near the resort, and he told us where to go, who to talk to, and how to get there. In fact, if we decided to go on Saturday morning, he would take us himself. Mark wasn't a travel agent. He was a travel *guide*. He had experienced the things we wanted to experience, and he could show us the best way to maximize our time. Sue could *teach*, but Mark could *show*. The right mentor can show you the way, not just teach it.

You can work to make the process of becoming mentored less intimidating. Sometimes you might think you're not quite ready to ask for help. Other times, you believe you can make it on your own. Even though both could be partly true, don't use them as excuses. Maybe you're afraid you'll be rejected and told, "Sorry, I just don't have the time to mentor you right now." But the very act of becoming mentored requires you to check your ego to begin with. And if you're going to prioritize memories over your ego, this commitment to being vulnerable in the process is the first step.

Next, to find the right mentor, you have to become a professional "fruit checker." Find someone with fruit on the tree who has the results you're hoping to attain. For example, if my goal is to lose fifty pounds, I wouldn't ask an overweight exercise coach to help me. If I wanted to be mentored by someone who could show me how to be a better husband, I wouldn't ask someone who has been divorced three times to tell me how to stay married. That would be like asking the classmate with a C- to tutor me in that same class.

I had a financial mentor when I was in my early twenties who had retired from his corporate job when he was just twenty-seven years old. He was my friend's dad, and I simply asked him one day if he ever mentored young adults. He knew about my ambitions in motorsports and saw my work ethic, and he agreed to mentor me to hit my financial goals to pursue my dreams.

The first thing he needed to see from me was where I had been spending my money for the last twelve months. I researched and categorized all my expenses and added up all the numbers. After looking at my income, expenses, and goals, he helped me develop a specific plan for the next six months to hit my targets. One of the agreements we made was that if anything would cost more than $100, we had to discuss the purchase first. I cut out all fast-food spending and created a smaller entertainment budget for the weekends. Some might say, "I can't believe you let someone else tell you when you can spend *your* money!" To those people I'd simply say, "Since I'm not on track to retire at twenty-seven years old like this guy did, maybe I should learn what he knows and apply his coaching."

I had to check my ego anytime I had a purchase that would cost more than $100. I would call him first to discuss whether it was something I really needed to buy or not. Start identifying someone who has positive results in the area where you're looking for guidance and begin by asking them if they ever mentor people. Then follow up their response by explaining why you hope they'd consider mentoring you, and simply ask if they would. Remember the cost of the things you don't yet know and be bold enough to ask for help.

Lastly, once you've found someone willing to mentor you, build the mentorship around asking the right questions. The greatest compliment you can give a mentor is asking good, thoughtful questions. To be fair, you might not always know the questions you should be asking. But it's worth noting that mentors find satisfaction and joy out of mentoring others, so they will be delighted to watch your light bulbs start to go off along the way.

Remember Jim, the SVP at my executive search firm? He pulled me aside one day after we'd had a few successful searches together and said, "Bryce, I like you because you ask a ton of questions . . . even the stupid ones!" I told him, "Thanks, but I'm a little paranoid that I don't know which ones were the stupid questions!" You should never be afraid of asking the *wrong* questions of your mentor—only be afraid of not asking *enough* questions. Asking enough questions will eventually lead you to asking the *right* ones. I have a friend who always says, "The stupidest questions are the ones you have but don't ask." There's something to be said about that, and I guess that's what I did. Good advice.

When someone is spending their time and effort to mentor you, they desire your success. They're enabling you to create more memories through growth. They're not there to make you feel better or to stroke their own ego by knowing more than you. They have immense value in helping you get where you want to go. Plus, you will develop a more meaningful relationship with a mentor than you previously thought. Think about it: I've already mentioned in here quite a few life lessons from my grandfather when he mentored me, and they're all extremely special memories. That's why finding a mentor is so critical. It enables you to shift into this gear of making more memories while limiting your ego to see your dreams happen.

TIME TRAVELER'S PERSPECTIVE

I'll be the first to admit that living life well can bear a physical and mental toll. Oftentimes, what you really need to prioritize in making memories is a shift in perspective: keep the bigger picture in the forefront of your mind. The question I'm asked most often when people find out I'm a professional Monster Jam driver is, "How hard is it being away from your family so much?" I miss my wife and kids like crazy when I'm on the road, but I've had to get intentional about how I spend that first day home after a trip. I'm usually extremely tired and sore when I walk in the door. After I give big hugs to the sweetest open arms a dad could ever ask for, I throw my gear bag in the designated spot in the laundry room, sit down on the couch, and the requests start flying at me.

"Dad, want to go outside and play soccer with us?" my kids will ask.

All I really want to do at that moment is sit on the couch, but I've found a tactic that helps me keep enough perspective and gets my butt up to go spend time with them. I imagine it's twenty years from now, and the kids are out on their own living their lives. At that future moment, I'm given the chance to time travel back to this exact day when my kids ask me to go outside and play soccer with them. If I had the chance to travel back in time to hear those sweet words come out of their mouths again, I know my future fifty-five-year-old self would give anything in the world for this chance. With that perspective, it's easy to respond with, "Yeah, buddy, go get your shoes on!" I'm told the days go by slowly, but the years go by fast. Maybe a time traveler's perspective is what you need most.

OUR FINEST TROPHIES

I recently introduced my five-year-old son, Keegan, to the world of BMX. He is still in the phase as a young kid where winning a shiny trophy is all he cares about. He wore the first medal he won around his neck for a week. He wouldn't leave home without it. In his mind, a trophy proved to everyone else that he's good at something and has what it takes to do cool stuff.

Imagine if, as his dad, all I cared about was that my kids were winning trophies for the same reasons. But when I see my kids do hard things or chase their dreams, I absolutely melt. Keegan can wear that medal all he wants because my mind immediately goes to standing at the top of that BMX starting box when I watched him drop onto the track for the first time completely unassisted. I've been less nervous competing on national television than I was letting him go down that twenty-foot hill. His ear-to-ear smile and immediate desire to do it again made me so proud it's hard to put into words. I want to raise confident kids. I want them to know they can accomplish whatever they set their minds to. And I don't know of a finer trophy than sharing those moments with them when they've pushed themselves past their comfort zones and done something that scared them.

While his physical trophies will surely meet their ultimate fate in a landfill like mine did, I look forward to the moments in twenty years when he and I reminisce about how much it meant to him when I stood there on the starting line cheering as he pushed the limits. And I will tell him how proud I was when I watched him, pass after pass, begin to believe in himself more and more. I can't imagine wanting anything more in my final moments on this earth than those memories to fill my heart and mind. Those will be my finest trophies, indeed!

While getting a good grade on an exam, landing that next promotion, getting the new house or car or bigger savings account might be the trophies you chase, all those things are fleeting. They aren't bad goals to have, but they should be attained to create more memories with the ones you love. Ace your exam so you can spend the weekend at the park with your brother instead of having to do extra credit to make up for the bad grade. Land the next promotion so you can quit your second job and spend more time with your family. Pay down that school debt to relieve stress levels with your spouse. But if all you have is a trophy to place on a mantle that doesn't create memories, you'll look around one day to realize your value is *replaceable*. It takes courage to set your sights on things that go against what our culture tells you is important. It requires boldness to give up the pursuit of the world's trophies to focus on things that are greater than yourself. The finest trophies you will cherish the most are the memories made along the way. Make them good ones!

TUNE-UP

1. What is your top ambition right now?
2. What will change in your life as a result of achieving this ambition? What will change in your loved ones' lives when you achieve it?
3. What would you choose if you could travel back in time to one day and relive a cherished moment? Why is that memory so special to you?

9

PIT CREW: 7TH GEAR

Become Built for Others

I once had the honor of being one of eight crew guys on my grandfather's Top Fuel drag racing team, turning wrenches on a 10,000-horsepower engine—before I even had a driver's license. At fifteen, I was our team's "clutch guy." My job was to rebuild the Top Fuel dragster's clutch between each pass the car made down the track. By the time we got the car back to our pit to begin the disassembly, the clutch's components were a scorching 1500°F.

I loved every second of thrashing on that race car through the years. Playing a part in helping my grandfather go from 0 to 300 mph in four seconds brought more happiness to me than most grandkids ever get to experience. Whenever Grandpa strapped into the car, I was always the final one to reach down into the cockpit, grip his hand, and tell him, "Go have fun!"

Top Fuel dragsters are so incredibly violent to experience in person that they register a 4 on the Richter scale (the scale that measures earthquakes) when they launch from the starting line. Once the car stops at the other end of the track, our team would jump in a vehicle to go retrieve it. Seeing the reaction on my grandfather's face after he'd just been shot out of a metaphorical cannon was priceless. He always had the biggest smile on his face. With his age, though, he usually needed my help getting out of the tight cockpit. I pulled up on his arm as he shifted his large frame upward. After a pass at Rockingham Dragway in 2007, I saw panic on his face when we met him at the end of the track.

"Nice job, Grandpa! How'd that run feel?" I asked him. No answer. I reached down into the cockpit to grab his arm and lift him up.

"*Wait! Wait! Wait!* I can't breathe! Get Mike!" He commanded. Mike was his son, crew chief, and my uncle.

"Mike! Grandpa needs you! Something's wrong!" I yelled.

Mike ran over. We thought Grandpa was out of breath, but he kept acting like he was breathing through a straw. We yelled over to the ambulance to get the medics. After five minutes, we lifted Grandpa up and out of the car and onto the stretcher. Nothing was helping him, and I saw a horrified look across his face that I'd never seen. They put him in the back of the ambulance and rushed him to the hospital. Our team got the race car back to our pit area, and then we rushed to the hospital.

When we arrived, we were met by the emergency room team who informed us just how bad off Grandpa was. He was unconscious when the ambulance reached the hospital, and his face had turned purple from lack of oxygen. Grandpa had been suffocating. He was experiencing heart failure, and fluid had backed up in his body and lungs as a result. The medical team administered amazing treatment to get his heart pumping again and saved his life that night. They said if he had arrived just a few minutes later, he wouldn't have survived.

What was meant to be a routine race pass that night turned into me almost losing my hero, and I was shaken by the experience. I still can't get out of my memory that look on his face when I reached him at the end of the track.

I loved turning wrenches on his Top Fuel dragster, but I never thought my duties as a crew guy would've included lifting my grandfather out of the car to save his life. I certainly didn't realize it would ultimately be the last race pass I'd ever get to watch him make. I wasn't there in the

1960s at the abandoned airstrip when he started racing, but I'm honored that I got to be part of his pit crew to help him chase his dream of driving a Top Fuel dragster. Helping him achieve that is a big reason I felt empowered to chase my own dreams.

Being a great crew person is about seeing a need and using your skills to fill that need. You, too, can serve as a crew member for the people in your life if you simply take your eyes off yourself long enough to see the assistance other people need to run their race. That's what being built for others is all about. It's born out of humility and engulfed in love for another person. We all want a pit crew in life that is there to help us fix the race car when it breaks down, but finding the right pit crew for ourselves starts with *becoming* a crew member for other people first. Learn how to support others, lift them up, and watch how many people decide to get behind you to help make your dreams happen.

CREWING FOR OTHERS

In 2013, I was in my two-year-old niece's hospital room when the doctor came in to give us an unfathomable diagnosis. Hannah had fallen at preschool and wouldn't stop crying from the pain in her back. After first going to the nearby hospital, she was sent to Brenner Children's Hospital in Winston-Salem, North Carolina, for further evaluation. Hannah finally fell asleep at Brenner's from the medication and her utter exhaustion from spending all afternoon in constant pain and undergoing multiple scans. As soon as the word "cancer" came out of the doctor's mouth a few hours later, Hannah's mom, Molly, started sobbing. We all stood there in disbelief. How is it possible that a child so young could have a softball-sized tumor on her kidney? How is a two-year-old expected to endure surgery, radiation, and chemotherapy?

Hannah later had her kidney removed where the Wilms tumor had attached itself. She endured grueling treatments for six months that left her body empty of strength and blood cells, but also, thankfully, empty of cancer. Today she's a happy twelve-year-old kid dealing with typical middle school drama, the only evidence of her cancer a surgical scar that she affectionately calls her "zipper."

Watching a nearly lifeless child is unimaginable. Yet there are always families across the world going through that horrific reality. According to the American Cancer Society as of June 23, 2023, cancer is the second leading cause of death, after accidents, in children ages 1 to 14. They also predict that nearly 1,040 children under the age of 15 will die from cancer in 2023.

As a professional Monster Jam driver, I've had the opportunity to meet a lot of families who have had their worlds turned upside down by cancer, just like my family experienced with my niece Hannah. The hardest thing about my career is getting to know a sick child who eventually dies from the affliction. It has happened more than anyone could've prepared me for, and it drives me to be a crew member for these families in two ways.

I use my platform to give these families breaks from their day-to-day struggles by facilitating real-life memories together. I also coordinate efforts through my fan base to crowdfund and raise money for specific needs I hear about. That's why I created our Live Like Warriors nonprofit (www.LiveLikeWarriors.com), where every dollar donated goes to the cause. We don't have staffing salaries to pay for printer ink or rent on a building. When a someone gives $10 in donations, it all goes to a specific family who has specific needs we want to fill. I've realized that, like me, donors love to know exactly where their gift is going and how their donation of any size will directly impact someone else.

This effort was born out of watching my niece go through her horrible cancer bout and seeing what her parents endured with hospital bills and emotional trauma as a result. I know that every family dealing with a sick child is also going through a lot. I've come to realize that most people who are willing to help don't know where or how to do it, so we show them the way. The good news is that we can be there to help through a coordinated effort and a volunteer army of givers. My vision is to have five thousand people become a part of the "Warrior Chain," through which we send out a message like the bat signal to Batman whenever a family's need arises, and we raise the funds within a few hours each time. If that sounds like something you'd want to be part of, visit our website and sign up! (www.LiveLikeWarriors.com)

❋ ❋ ❋

When we get unstuck in life, shifting out of neutral and through the different gears outlined in this book, something interesting starts to happen. Oftentimes we're so preoccupied with fixing our own lives that we can't imagine taking our eyes off the past-due bills or the frustrating situation at school or work long enough to help someone else in need. But shifting into this gear of becoming built for others puts us in a position to take our experiences, even the bad ones, and turn them into fuel for other people. We become the gas can for the motorist stranded on the highway, or the anonymous note that empowers someone to stay positive for one more day. We become the fuel that ignites change in this world.

I used to think that people with a noble cause were just smarter or kinder than I was. Sure, I was never closed off to helping people, but I didn't really know where to start. A message from someone on social media prompted my first mental click of how I could take my experiences and platform in Monster Jam and use them to become built for others. It started from an idea for collecting Legos for a kid named Ollie.

WARRIOR OLLIE

I love getting messages on social media from families who love Monster Jam. Most of the messages are fun to get, but others are quite difficult to read. One message a few years ago from the aunt of a little boy named Ollie fell into the latter category. She shared how Ollie was going through treatment for a rare form of cancer called embryonal rhabdomyosarcoma. While losing his hair from chemotherapy, he nicknamed himself "Mohawk Warrior." His dad had given him one of my die-cast trucks to encourage him. Before all his hair fell out, he asked his mom to cut what was left into a mohawk so he could be the real "Mohawk Warrior" for a day. I was gutted.

I found out that Ollie liked to build with Legos to help pass the time in the hospital, so I figured the monster truck community might want to step in as his motivational pit crew for a moment by sending him a few Lego sets. I put out the word and was overwhelmed by the number of Lego sets that were sent. I had so many to give Ollie that it was less expensive to drive them all to Nashville (where he lived) myself than to ship them. I was looking for an excuse to meet this real-life warrior anyway. His parents loved the idea of surprising him.

When I arrived, Ollie was a bit shell-shocked. With every single Lego set he unwrapped, he ran through the house and jumped off the furniture with reckless abandonment. He forgot he had cancer at that moment and became a normal kid again.

Ollie found the strength to keep battling until he was given the good news that he was officially cancer-free. He has to show no signs of cancer for five years to officially be in remission, but he's already moved on to his next challenge. He's an upcoming star in the BMX world today. He still wears a helmet with a mohawk on it like a warrior's medal. A group of strangers decided to become crew members for Ollie by sending a $15 Lego set and putting a smile on that kid's face. They showed love to a family who needed to be reminded that they had more support than they realized from people they'd never met. That's what being built for others looks like.

BECOMING BUILT FOR OTHERS

As I drove seven hours home to North Carolina after leaving Ollie, I thought about how easy and rewarding it had been to bless a kid and encourage a family during their battle. I thought about my approach to becoming one of Ollie's crew members for an afternoon and asked myself three key questions to determine if I had given him my best effort. I now believe these are the key questions to answer if we're going to become great crew members for others:

- Did I leave things better than I found them?
- Did I lighten someone's load?
- Did I see them as their best version?

Did I leave things better than I found them?

Back in high school when I was restoring my 1970 Mustang Mach 1, I had to have a mechanical inspection to register it in North Carolina. The horn wasn't working on the steering wheel, which would have made the car fail the inspection. Instead of dealing with the car's whole wiring harness under the dash and chasing down the correct wires, I decided to add a separate horn button just to pass the inspection until I had time to do the job right. I took the car to a shop in town and asked them to install it. Big mistake.

A 1970 fully restored American muscle car is valuable and keeps increasing in value each year it ages. Any real mechanic would relish the chance to turn a wrench on one. The mechanic I hired opened the hood, ran the horn button wires from the dash to the engine bay, and then to the front of the grill where the horn was located. He then realized the wires were short by about three inches. Instead of starting over and running longer wires, he physically bent the horn itself to make the short wires connect. While it made the horn button work, he damaged the original component and decreased the car's value. I was flabbergasted. He left the components in worse shape than he had found them.

Something so simple spoke volumes to me about how little value that shop placed on a classic car. Yet how many times have I taken the same approach to dealing with people in my life? How many times have I taken the easy path with others rather than spend a few extra minutes to find a way to add value to their lives? People who make a positive impact always leave things *better* than they found them, not worse. They bring value. They *never* reduce it.

In his book *They Call Me Coach*, legendary basketball coach John Wooden said:

> Many building custodians across the country would tell you that UCLA left the shower and dressing room the cleanest of any team. We picked up all the tape, never was there soap on the shower floor for someone to slip on, made sure all the showers were turned off, and all towels were accounted for. The towels were always deposited in a receptacle, if there was one, or stacked neatly near the door. It seems to me that this is everyone's responsibility—not just the manager's. Furthermore, I believe it is a form of discipline that should be a way of life, not to please some building custodian, but as an expression of courtesy and politeness that each of us owes to his

fellow man. These little things establish a spirit of togetherness and consideration that help unite the team into a solid unit.

Leaving a locker room clean is one thing, but what about bringing value to everyday life? I started to keep track of how often I'd start a workday with the goal of bringing as much value as possible. The results weren't great at first. But if I had a superpower, it would be this: I recognize that there is a season for everything. I won't always have my name up in lights as a professional Monster Jam driver. One day, this chapter of life will end for me. The question I'm always asking myself is, "Am I going to leave Monster Jam better than I found it?" That drives me to work harder when I'm exhausted. It also reminds me that we never arrive at the pinnacle, regardless of our position. There is always more to be done because there will always be more people to add value to.

That afternoon with Ollie allowed me to leave him and his family better than I found them with a renewed energy to face his next cancer treatment. If you can have the mindset of leaving things (and people) better than you found them, you will finally start shifting into a gear of being built for others and leave a lasting impact on their lives.

Did I lighten someone's load?

I walked into my living room one morning, and my wife, McKenzie, was crying. I knew something was wrong. She gathered herself long enough to tell me there had been an accident in Jamaica where her dad was leading a high school mission trip, which was something they had done for more than twenty years without serious incident.

My father-in-law and the others were at a swimming hole on their day off when a large branch fell out of the trees and hit both Paul (my father-in-law) and one of the other leaders, twenty-six-year-old Lee Rickman, in the head. Lee died almost instantly and nobody knew if my father-in-law was going to make it.

We immediately drove out to Paul's house here in North Carolina to formulate a plan. We couldn't get any answers about Paul because he was in the hospital separated from the group at that point. The high school had three chaperones leading this group of about fifteen students. One was dead, one was in a Jamaican hospital, and the third was dealing with the aftermath. All the students had witnessed the accident.

There were no ambulances in Jamaica to rush to the scene like we have in America. Two of the group's Jamaican guides grabbed Lee and took off toward the hospital in the back of a taxi. It was being driven so fast that it blew the motor on the way, coasted into a police station, where they got out of the taxi and got into a different vehicle to finish the drive to the hospital. Lee never regained consciousness and was pronounced dead at the hospital.

It was beyond traumatic for the students, and the atmosphere back home was devastating. No one knew what to do. The original return flights were booked for a few days from then, but after the students went through that type of situation, they couldn't be left in another country to deal with the trauma. Our family needed to get to Paul to make sure he was OK and bring him back stateside. Lee's family had to deal with getting Lee's body home. As our family scrambled, it turned out that my mother-in-law and I were the only ones who had valid passports at the time. We immediately bought plane tickets and left on the next flight.

On the way to the airport, I called Scott Reitnour, my former soccer coach from high school, who had coached both Lee and me at Wesleyan Academy. I asked Scott, "What the heck am I supposed to do when I get down there? They've all been through something so traumatic. Maybe I'm the wrong person to be going into this situation." Scott was still shaken up from the news of Lee's death, but he calmly responded with instructions that have stuck with me in times of crisis ever since. He said, "Bryce, the only thing you're supposed to do for them is serve. Find any possible way to serve in any capacity you can. Even if you just get a cup of water for someone, don't stop serving until you get them all back home."

I thought about his advice the entire plane ride down to Jamaica, and I had a distinct vision of Lee's backpack. I didn't want any of the students to have to carry Lee's backpack to North Carolina and hand it to his family. For some reason, I knew that would be a traumatic moment, and they'd all been through enough already. I wanted to lighten the load for those students both physically and emotionally by carrying the backpack myself. I cried the night before we flew home from Jamaica when I gathered his things. I sat on his bed alone, staring at his stuff in disbelief that any of this could have happened. By the way, remember the freshman teammate I yelled at in the last chapter for being more competitive than me back in high school? That was Lee. Now I was the one shedding tears.

Paul was still in the hospital, but he was conscious and recovering. One of the only times I've seen my father-in-law cry was when we finally got to his hospital bed and my mother-in-law grabbed his arm. I don't think she left his side until they were back home a few days later.

When we made it back to the States and started walking up that terminal in Greensboro, North Carolina, the brave faces the students had mustered for the previous few days disappeared instantly. They saw their parents crying with arms wide open, and they all broke into a full-out sprint with cries I knew would only be comforted by their parents.

The moment I had dreaded the most—handing Lee's backpack to his family—had arrived. I broke down as I gave the backpack to Lee's two brothers. His brother Matt said in disbelief, "He should've been walking up that terminal just now with you guys." The worst pain someone can experience is losing a loved one, and I can't imagine losing a son or a brother in such a traumatic way.

The truth is, we interact with people everyday who have been through trauma. Life is messy. Serving others, no matter how big or how small the act, starts with seeing others' pain and desiring their relief from it. Being in someone's pit crew sometimes means carrying their backpack to lighten their load, and to "not stop serving until you get them home."

Did I see them as their best version?

When we enter the "real world" after graduating high school, we think we're invincible. I quickly found out that pursuing a dream is like grabbing a tiger by the tail. There are so many unknown dynamics that arise and try to convince us we don't have what it takes to achieve our dream. The darkest point of my life came after yet another obstacle arose to try and keep me from realizing my dream of being a professional race car driver. I was past the point of questioning myself. I didn't believe I could achieve it anymore. The darkness crept over me when I stopped believing that anyone else could accomplish their dreams either. "What's the point of any of us trying to avoid an average life?" I would reason. I started to see any person who had accomplished their dream as just a fluke. They were lucky. Privileged. And every other excuse I could come up that let me sleep at night in my bed of self-induced failure.

I was never arrogant enough to think I could find success as a "one-man band." But after my planned-for career in professional drag racing ended in 2011, I became so narcissistic and judgmental that I began to repel others. I stopped seeing people at their best, and I began to hope they didn't have what it took to succeed either. I found myself serving others less and lecturing them more. I started finding ways to take instead of give because it all felt like a wasted effort.

That level of selfishness was a cancer to my soul, and I felt like I would wilt away. I was being the opposite of a person of influence. I was acting like I was built only for myself and for an average life. Thankfully, I had a mentor who took hold of my arm and shined a big flashlight into my darkness.

My high school soccer coach's name is Scott, but I still call him Coach to this day because of what he has meant to me during some of the most critical years of my life. He was the first coach who saw me for my strengths instead of trying to subdue my weaknesses. He empowered me like a charging port in my chest during high school. Then, after I failed at a career in professional drag racing, he invited me to come out to his soccer practices for a few weeks.

He never lectured me about getting back on my feet. He never told me to stop whining. He simply put me into a coaching role where he leveraged my skills to get me back into a mode of seeing the impact I'm capable of making. He used my passion for winning and mentoring others to develop his players. He had me talk about my experiences to the team, and I watched as these teenagers responded. I might not have been giving them the secrets to life at that point, but I noticed that they were drawn to my passion. I could serve them both on and off the field by simply showing my enthusiasm for the game of soccer and for becoming a leader. Coach was a crew member for my life when I needed someone to see me as my best version instead of my worst.

You have to believe that other people in your life need you to be this same type of crew member for them. If you make the shift to becoming built for others, you start to realize how much value you can bring to someone else in this world. It's important to get out of neutral, shift back into motion, learn to work as hard as possible for the things you want most in life, and focus on the right finish lines. But nothing will bring you more satisfaction and meaning than the giving of yourself to make someone else's life better. Yes, you need to learn how to use your skill set to find another gear in life you never knew you had. But the best confirmation of your worth will be when you realize how much value you can add if you have the courage to shift into becoming built for others.

PASSIONATE HUMILITY

During my driving career, I've had mostly great crew members. What separated the great ones from the average ones was the consistent use of an attribute they brought with them. It wasn't their technical abilities. It wasn't their knowledge of the machinery or tools. It wasn't their preventative maintenance practices. All those elements are important. But the attribute that the best crew possessed was passionate humility.

When a driver and crew are both passionately humble—meaning they constantly look for ways to learn and perform better with a vigorous mentality—they form a harmonious relationship where everyone progresses into the best version of themselves. They also see each *other* as the best version instead of pointing fingers of blame or accusation. If all a crew member brings to the table is technical ability, he or she usually gets comfortable and stops progressing. When people are is passionately humble, however, they take so much pride in their product that they constantly look for ways to execute better for the sake of the team. All the components mentioned above are automatically covered as a result. Passionately humble people look for ways to serve and bring value to the situation and to those around them. They bring a fire in their bellies that burns with a desire to become the best.

Maybe you have no plans of becoming an actual crew member for a race team, but becoming built for others requires the same thing. Like my grandfather's near-death experience at the end of the racetrack, many people in our world are experiencing some form of heart failure of their own, and they need us to reach down, grab them by the arm, and lift them out of their situation. When you find and fill the needs of others with a passionate humility, you don't make the interaction about yourself. You don't seek recognition. You don't require reward.

You believe you can leave things better than you found them, that you can lighten someone's load, and that the people you interact with are worth serving. When you approach the needs of others with this same vigorous mentality, you can find another gear you never knew you had. You can finally be the desperately needed crew member for someone else and start having the impact you've always believed you could have. And if nothing else, you might just be the key to someone out there having those critical wrenches turned on their lives that enable them to finally start winning again. Isn't that worth it all?

THE FINAL RIDE: BECOMING A FARMER

The weekend following my Albuquerque anxiety-related medical debacle, I had never been so excited to interact with our fans and strap into a truck. You may think I would've been timid, but I had shifted into a new gear when I became driven by my beliefs once again. I also started winning a lot more. But I wasn't nearly as concerned with that part of the journey showing results as I had been previously.

My new outlook—believing that good things were coming around the next corner—was causing me to make the type of impact I had always dreamed of. You've perhaps heard that people who've had a near-death experience often say things like, "That made me realize what was most important in this life!" What they're doing is falling back on a belief that time is our most valuable asset.

That next weekend at Monster Jam brought so many moments of gratitude to me that I began to see all the things I had been missing out on when I was only focusing on winning. I hadn't previously realized just how great of a chance I had to inspire the next generation to chase their dreams. I started to view these families coming through my autograph line as seeds of greatness. I had the opportunity to speak good things over people, to make them feel loved and appreciated, and to encourage them. I became a farmer who planted and cultivated these seeds of greatness in hopes they would eventually sprout into the best versions of themselves.

The greatest shift in my life has been becoming built for others. Making that shift drove me to start our Live Like Warriors organization (www.LiveLikeWarriors.com) where, as I mentioned earlier, we engage our fan base to crowdfund specific needs in the world. Helping others motivated me to create online content and to write this book. Most importantly, it made me remember that one of these events will be my last in a Monster Jam truck. One of those thirty-foot jumps, one of those backflips, one of those freestyle runs will be my last chance to make an impact through this platform.

I choose to believe that when I make that final ride, I'll be able to look back with gratitude that I was given the opportunity to impact the world through motorsports. I've never regretted becoming built for others. My only regrets are reserved for the time I wasted allowing the pressure of uncontrollable results to shape my selfish decisions in life. I believe your impact can also be greater than you ever dreamed. Will you *become built for others* with me?

TUNE-UP

1. Past or present, who would you say has been a "crew member" for you? Describe them.
2. Regardless of whether you think you can help fill it or not, what is a need for your family/friends/community right now? Who could use some financial assistance today? Who needs to receive an encouraging text?
3. Do you think people would describe you as "passionate," "humble," or both? If not both, what could you change about how you interact with others to become more "passionately humble"?

10

THE LAST RUN

Make It Count

"What is your most prized possession?" That was a question on the Monster Jam driver profile questionnaire. I really struggled giving an answer. The truth is, the older I get, the less value I place on material items. Sure, the stuff hanging on the walls in my shop would all be personally meaningful enough to give as an answer. The 1970 Mustang Mach 1 that I now consider an heirloom would certainly qualify as one of my most valuable possessions. But what would I say is my absolute most prized possession? It is a painting.

Now, I'm not much of an art guy. I get skeptical when I hear someone describe a painting by saying things like,

"Wow, that art really speaks to me." At the absolute most, a Bob Ross landscape painting *might* make me feel calmer. But maybe it's his sultry voice that brings the good vibes—shout-out to all the "happy little trees" out there.

The painting I have is called *Night Wing II—The Last Run* by a motorsports artist named Kenny Youngblood. It was a tribute painting to the famous drag racing pioneer, "Big Daddy" Don Garlits. If you search for it online, you'll see that it's a painting from the vantage point of standing behind a Top Fuel dragster with its eight-foot-high exhaust flames shooting into the night air. It has incredibly vivid colors and such realistic paint strokes that it feels like the canvas is shaking off the wall. It was the last thing my grandfather ever gave me before he died. It was as if he were passing the torch to me, and we both burst into tears as he handed it to me.

The painting now sits in a prominent place in my house as a constant reminder that someday we will all make our "last run." One day will be our last chance to put the helmet on, to high-five a fan, to celebrate with our team after an event, to make a memory with our family, and to make a difference doing something bigger than ourselves. But this painting really depicts any person with a dream or passion who desires to live a life above average. Whatever endeavor you choose will require you to shift into different gears every step of the way in order to fulfill your potential and make the biggest impact possible before you make your *last run*.

FOCUSING ON THE NEXT SHIFT

Quite frankly, it would be nearly impossible to get all these gears right all the time. But this book isn't about getting all this stuff correct. It's about having the courage and patience to know which of these gears you need to shift into when life throws a wrench at you.

As I've wrestled with these gears while writing this book, I've been thinking, "If this was the last message I ever got to leave my kids, what would I write?"

I'm absolutely gutted to think my kids are going to go through discouragement, confusion, hopelessness, anger, exhaustion, and searching for answers. Everyone goes through those things, and likely more. I just know how lonely and lost it can feel to figure out this crazy thing called life. The great news is that there will be an entire group of people waiting on the other side of our comfort zones for those willing to do whatever it takes not to succumb to a "normal life." The journey might feel lonely at times, but there are people you will meet along the way who harbor the same ambition and desire to make an impact. They'll be standing on the fence line cheering as you make *your* last run.

I don't regret the hard stuff, the late hours, the rejections, or the uncertainties. I regret that life doesn't always allow us to enjoy the mountaintops and the valleys with the people we want to be there with us. My grandfather was my hero, but he's not here anymore to give me counsel when I've been angry, exhausted, or lost in different seasons of this journey.

But just because you feel alone at times doesn't mean you don't have a pit crew supporting you in the background. Sometimes the best support system consists of the lessons you've already learned from previous disappointments—when you gained the counsel you need to keep shifting through your gears. You may not always make the *right* shift, but you can commit to making your *next* shift as you strive to become your best version.

CRASH COURSE

I am incredibly grateful for so many late nights in the race shop and long road trips when I heard my grandfather talk about being geared for life. He didn't just teach me foundational beliefs, though. I watched him make difficult decisions based on what he believed, not on what was convenient. Then he walked beside me and helped me make important shifts during my teen years and into adulthood. He empowered me to stand on my own and make my own shifts as a man today.

I'm struck by three moments with him, three stories I often tell that paint a clear picture of how he took me through this crash course of becoming geared for life. It wasn't a secret formula he shared with me. He first taught me by example what shifting into a gear looks like. Then he walked beside me as we shifted gears together. And he watched me as I shifted on my own.

Watch Me Shift

I watched my grandfather shift into the gear of making a memory with me instead of feeding his ego. He was always coming up with ways to do things for his grandkids when we'd hit certain ages—like buying us our own go-kart when we turned eight years old. I'll never forget thinking that buying me a go-kart was the coolest thing in the world, until I drove it straight into the barn.

Now, I want to be clear: this was an eighty-acre farm. The barn wasn't exactly in a tight corner on the property. It was on the wide-open part of the land. I was driving around the farm and decided to hit the gas pedal full throttle, which was when I rammed it into the side of the wooden barn. I cried like I had just broken every bone in my body, when in fact I had simply jammed my finger and damaged my ego. I was so embarrassed. My grandfather worked hard for everything he got, and he had every right to be mad that I damaged both the barn and my new go-kart. But I'll never forget how Grandpa came and checked on me after someone carried me back to the house.

My grandfather was a man's man. A pioneer. A dad to four of the manliest men I've still ever met in my life, and a daughter (my mother) who embodies the word *strength.* You would think he would be this sort of rough, callous, testosterone-breathing guy who wouldn't have put up with such carelessness as me driving into his barn. But he came to me, looked me in the eye with genuine concern, and cared about me. Based on my hysteria, he was probably making sure I wouldn't be paralyzed for life.

Instead of telling me to quit crying so he could inspect the damage, he joked with me. He turned and announced he would be going to grab his chainsaw and would return to cut off my thumb, which was propped up on an ice pack. I remember being about 60 percent sure he was kidding, but

I couldn't risk the other 40 percent. I pleaded with him not to chainsaw off my thumb. He thankfully obliged, and then he asked me if I wanted him to cut down the barn instead. Even as an eight-year-old, I realized in that moment that he wasn't putting the blame on me, even though he could have easily lectured me for my reckless driving and childlike reaction to the situation. That was all I needed to hear. The tears stopped. I also began pleading for the very life of the barn because I didn't want him to chainsaw it to pieces in my honor. He chose to shift into the gear of making a memory with me by playfully overreacting to the chaos I had created, and I'm very grateful for it.

I'll Help You Shift

It's not easy getting a teenager to engage and start understanding what it looks like to shift into a gear he doesn't realize he has. However, Grandpa managed to do that with me at the racetrack when I was just fourteen years old, when he invited me to thrash at my first Top Fuel drag racing national event. I wanted to tag along and clean the car since I thought it was cool. He agreed to let me clean it and help a crew guy on the bottom end of the motor fetch wrenches. I'm 100 percent sure I was in the way, but nobody said anything.

We qualified for the race and lost in the second round, but I had never worked so hard in my entire life. We got our hearts broken in the second round after the dragster made a violent move and apparently scraped the concrete barrier at 295 mph. However, after they disqualified us for hitting the wall, nobody (including the tech officials) could find a mark on the dragster. We said, "Guys, if we hit a concrete wall at nearly 300 mph, don't you think it would leave a mark?" We pleaded with them to show us a scrape or a mark, and they started to agree that they would remove the disqualification from our run. But as they were walking away, the official noticed a small half-inch scrape on the outer edge of the rear rim. We couldn't believe it, but the proof was right there. We threw up our hands in surrender and sat down to catch our breath from the thrash of the day.

After we spent the next three hours packing up the trailer, I fell asleep in a lawn chair waiting for the green light to hit the road back to the shop. Then I slept the entire ten-hour drive back on the floor of our motorhome and slept another eight hours after we pulled in the driveway. That's eighteen hours of sleep. My grandfather came up to me the next day and handed me a $100 check, which I refused. He pleaded that I take it and said, "You physically emptied yourself with our team, and you don't know how much that meant to me." I looked back at him and said, "But I did that for you, Grandpa," with tears in my eyes.

He made me take the check. I wish I had kept it and never deposited it, but $100 feels like $100,000 when you're fourteen years old. I've hung on to that feeling ever since. He taught me how to find the gear of emptying myself with a work ethic I'm still able to shift into today when I'm chasing my dreams.

Now You Shift, and I'll Watch

Lastly, Grandpa equipped and empowered me to start making my own shifts in life the night I made my first full pass in the driver's seat of his Top Fuel dragster. I had envisioned driving a Top Fuel dragster every day of my life from the time I was thirteen years old until I got to drive it at twenty-one. Somehow, I convinced him to let me use his $250,000 race car to get my Top Fuel license. We went to (what is now) Kentucky Dragway in Clay City, Kentucky, where I grew up drag racing, to complete my first few passes. This was as special as it gets for me. This was where I first saw a Top Fuel dragster go down the track at the hands of my grandfather, who had set the track record a few years earlier.

My first race pass didn't go well. As soon as I punched the throttle, I also managed to pull the parachutes. I didn't go sixty feet on my first-ever Top Fuel pass without looking like an absolute amateur. That was what you call a "face-palm" moment. I thought I'd look at my grandfather and he'd have utter disappointment on his face. But no, he was all smiles and asked me how the first sixty feet felt. Amazing. Great sense of humor, that guy. The motor on a Top Fuel car has to be completely disassembled after every single pass. We still had to disassemble the entire motor after my mistake. Still, he was all smiles and eating peanut butter cookies while mixing fuel for our next run.

Fast forward to the last pass of the day—we were going for my first full eighth of a mile run. It was nighttime, the lights were up, and a nice cool October evening breeze was blowing. I was strapped in and waiting for the signal from the track for our crew to start up the 10,000-horsepower engine sitting twenty-four inches behind my head, when my grandfather leaned into the cockpit, grabbed my arm, prayed that God would be glorified that night through our efforts, and then said to me, "I believe in you, buddy. Make it count!" He was releasing me onto the track on my own in an incredibly dangerous vehicle. But he knew I had chosen to shift into my gear of being purpose driven and that I had chosen this path of motorsports to see it come to fruition.

I managed to run the full eighth of a mile, not hitting anything on the way, and resetting the track record Grandpa had set just a few years earlier. I was delirious. It was one of the best experiences of my life. But even better than the feeling of getting shot out of a cannon or setting the track record was what happened when I got back to the pit area. My grandfather leaned into the cockpit, tapped my chest with his finger, and told me he was proud of me with tears in his eyes. I had envisioned that moment since I was thirteen. I burst into tears.

Many people have not had that kind of grandfatherly figure in their lives. What my grandfather did for me is what I hope this book will do for you: empower and equip you to become geared for life. Grandpa wasn't a normal guy, and he never tried to chase after average things. He was the type of guy who made everyone around him better. My advantage over most people is that I had someone in my life who was willing to show me, help me, and then watch me shift into different gears in hopes of maximizing my full potential.

The good news is that if you apply the gears in this book, you'll eventually become that positive influence and equip others to become geared for life as well. No matter the stall outs, burnouts, pressures, or resistance you face, let this book serve as that shift point into your full potential. This world needs you to find the courage to step out and become your best version. As I lean into your cockpit before you hit the track and run your race, shifting through your gears to accelerate to new speeds previously thought impossible, becoming built for others and making ridiculously cool memories along the way, I want you to know that I believe in you! Make it count! You were made for such a time as this. You've got what it takes. Now go live the life you've always wanted and leave this world better than you found it.

TUNE-UP

1. Have you prioritized your comfort zone over your potential?
2. Who do you hope is standing on the fence line cheering you on as you make your *last run*?
3. What is the next shift you need to make to become geared for life?

EPILOGUE

The Finish Line

Before we part ways, I want to share a secret ingredient for what it really looks like to be geared for life. The difference between living an average life and living a life at your fullest potential isn't intelligence or luck. It is *urgency*. Knowing you don't have unlimited time to make your impact should cause your feet to hit the ground in the morning with some pep in your step. Crossing the finish line of life is inevitable, but you get to decide how you approach it.

Earlier in life as I was working my guts out trying to make my professional drag racing dream happen, I had a litmus test I'd use every night while lying in bed. I'd simply ask myself, "If I could relive today, would I?" Most days are filled with monotony that leave us feeling devoid of meaning and would force us to answer "probably not." When you wake up after hitting the snooze button three times, grab a muffin while heading out the door late for work, survive eight hours at a job you don't enjoy, come home to a microwaved plate of food to eat before binge-watching another season of a streamed show, you might not feel much desire to relive those unmemorable days.

The great days, when you *feel* something—when you get to live out your purpose or help another person live out theirs, or maybe make a really great memory with the people you love—are the days you will wish you could experience again and multiply. Those are the days during which you will find the most traction. Those are the days you find the right gear to propel you. If you had more of those days than the monotonous ones, living a life to your fullest potential would be inevitable. But recognizing that your days are numbered—whether great days of traction or monotonous days—should drive you not to wait for someone to give you permission to become the best version of yourself.

MAKING THE DASH COUNT

On one of the last road trips we took together, Grandpa turned off the highway unexpectedly while we were heading to a race. We drove about a mile east until we came to a cemetery. Believe it or not, this wasn't the strangest detour he had ever taken. I sat silently for a minute as I waited for him to explain why we were there. Did he have some family member buried here that I was unaware of? Could it be a distant aunt whose gravesite he wanted to visit? I climbed out of the race rig and walked a few acres by his side, neither one of us saying much at all. When we got to the middle, he stopped and asked me, "Bryce, what do you see?"

"Uh, graves. Some trees over there. Flowers someone left." I answered as if we were playing the creepiest game of "I Spy" ever created.

"No. What do you see at each grave?" he said.

"Just gravestones," I answered.

"What's on them?"

"Their names. When they were born and died. A small description of them." I was running out of answers.

As if he were doing all this just to remind himself why we were there, Grandpa finally said, "Bryce, the majority of potential to walk this earth ends up buried in cemeteries just like this one. Most people never choose to realize they have seeds of greatness inside them. The most important thing on that gravestone isn't the birth date or the death date. The only thing that matters is the dash in the middle. We gotta make the dash count."

Are you making your dash count? If not, it's time for you to start shifting gears. If you can find the courage to shift into that next gear, that effort will never come back void. You have what it takes to make a difference and create your own ripple effects. You can become the difference maker your family deserves when you commit to living for something bigger than yourself. Your secret to creating a life worth living is having a *last run* mentality—knowing you won't have an infinite number of chances to make your dreams happen. You don't have time to blame your failures, your situation, or your past. That is a waste of time, energy, and thought, and it won't help you shift into a gear you never knew you had. If you spend half as much time believing in yourself as you do doubting yourself, your whole life will change.

These gears will open you up to the *best* version of yourself, the best version you've ever been, and maybe a version you can't even see right now. You can find your purpose again, and it might not look like whatever purpose you had before. You can become someone who chooses to believe in possibilities instead of being rooted in doubt. You can start making memories instead of egos. You can become built for others. You can face pressure and obstacles and keep accelerating. And because of all of this, you'll be willing to empty yourself in the process, to thrash and refill your tank and keep moving forward.

Once you start seeing the best version of yourself, you won't be able to go back. Are you the finished product today that you want to be? No, of course not. None of us are. But your strength will become based on your ability to shift into the gear you need when life's journey goes off track. Once you understand how to shift and what gear to shift into, you'll be unstoppable. You won't have regrets on your deathbed because you'll be proud that you were willing to keep moving. You'll be proud of your journey. Can you imagine *that*?

Imagine right now that you're blessed enough to grow old. You're sitting with your adult kids at the family dinner table where you've shared a lot of meals. You start talking about life after you're gone—maybe what's in your will, your final wishes on burial, what to do with that classic car in the garage. Those things embody memories that talk about lessons learned and moments of comfort for you. The conversation quickly shifts to your kids telling stories about their childhood. In those moments, they'll all be good memories.

Imagine next your kids starting to talk about the hard moments where they knew life was being tough on you. That time you were laid off. The sorrow they saw you experience when your brother passed. They tell you how they learned resiliency through watching you turn your pain into purpose during your bout with cancer when you began counseling others going through the same battle. They tell the story about when you worked a second job to pay for the neighbors to live in a hotel for three months after their house burned down. They share memories of you giving up that work event to be with them at home for family movie night amid that potential promotion. They remember how a stranger was aggressive with them at a baseball game in the parking lot, and you totally calmed the situation (and they finish the story with, "That guy was lucky he backed off, because you would've knocked him out!"). They tell the story about how they knew your boss was pushing you to do things you didn't believe were right, so you chose to leave the company, and that meant your family had to eat tuna for dinner every night until you found another job (they laugh and admit they still can't stand the smell of tuna). They talk about the time they knew your new business venture was struggling, but you never missed a morning of giving thanks for having a heartbeat and declaring positive emotion over the possibilities of the coming day.

They tell endless stories about how you were the hardest worker they'd ever known. They talk about loving the scar on your right hand that you got from the fence posts you placed in the backyard so they could finally get that English bulldog they'd nagged you about for years. They joke about how hard you snored in your recliner in the family room after pouring yourself into chasing your dreams all day. They say they learned to empty their tanks in their own pursuits from watching you.

That moment will make all the effort, the hardships, the unknowns worth it. The peace you exude will be palpable. Having your loved ones become inspired because you constantly chose to take more risks, have more faith, and be creative enough to keep shifting gears along the way will be your exclamation point. That will be your *last run*. The people you positively influenced will be by your side, ready to carry your legacy forward and make an impact of their own. You just have to be willing to find that next gear, make that next shift, and change the world.

Are you ready to make your dash count?

See you at the finish line.
Bryce Kenny

ACKNOWLEDGMENTS

This book never would have been written without a constant prodding to start from my brother Rhett. Thank you for pushing me to find this gear as an author—a gear I never knew I had. Your encouragement was invaluable. Also, for our intense ping-pong battles growing up that gave me confidence knowing I could occasionally beat you at something.

To the best kids in the world, Eliza, Keegan, and Ava, for giving me more purpose to my days. The three of you put breath in my lungs and make me want to shift into my best version. And, yes, you can go get another snack.

To my wife, McKenzie, for always believing that this book's message was worth writing and that I had what it took to author it. You are my prayer warrior, my lover, and my friend. Life would be impossible without you. Now it's your turn to write your own book that I believe will change the world. Don't let me be the only author in our household!

To Jason Watts, Brian Staples, Matt Moger, Tony Mancini, Janet Coates, Lisa Hake, and Doug Kershaw, thank you for your invaluable feedback and suggestions. Your input made all the difference and gave me the confidence to move forward with this book. I owe each of you a steak dinner.

To Mom, for always being my biggest cheerleader and for your willingness to beat up the haters who have dared to cross your third (and favorite) son! To Dad, for always telling me you are proud of me, except on the golf course.

To the entire team at Dexterity, and notably to Matt West, for driving the process forward to turn this book into something great. We took a jagged, dirty, dangerous rock and polished it into a smooth, beautiful, and dynamic stone together. And thank you, Dave Schroeder, for the wisdom in connecting me with such an amazing publishing group.

To everyone at Feld Entertainment and the entire Great Clips organization, thank you for believing in me and allowing me to live this insanely cool life as a Monster Jam driver. And to the entire motorsports community, you are the reason God put me on this earth. Somewhere out there is a kid standing at the track's fence line watching you chase your dreams and looking for the courage to chase his or her own. I look forward to shifting gears with all of you to make the biggest impact on this world that we can.

NOTES

p. 93. *Stu Weber* wrote. Stu Weber, *Tender Warrior*, (New York: Multnomah Books, 2006), 221.

pp. 114–115. *Man's Search for Meaning*. Viktor E. Frankl, *Man's Search for Meaning: The Classic Tribute to Hope from the Holocaust* (London: Rider, 2004), 115.

p. 133. *Psychologist and media commentator.* Joe Rogan and Jordan Peterson, "Joe Rogan Experience #1070 - Jordan Peterson," January 30, 2018, produced by Joe Rogan, podcast, 1:08:08, https://www.jrepodcast.com/episode/joe-rogan-experience-1070-jordan-peterson/.

p. 134. *What I needed.* John C. Maxwell, *The 21 Irrefutable Laws of Leadership: Follow Them and People Will Follow You* (Nashville: Thomas Nelson, 1998), 16.

pp. 176–177. *In his book.* John Wooden, with Jack Tobin, *They Call Me Coach* (New York: McGraw-Hill Education, 2004) 104.

ABOUT THE AUTHOR

Bryce Kenny is a big kid who never gave up on his dream of a career in motorsports. In addition to being a Monster Jam driver, he is a fan of drag racing and monster trucks. For over two decades, Bryce has worked as a professional in the motorsports industry, even setting a Guinness World Record for top speed in a monster truck. In recent years, Bryce has become an inspirational speaker, sharing his uplifting message with millions of people who need the courage to take bold steps in their own lives. He is the author of *Geared for Life,* a book that guides readers to becoming unstuck in life and finding that gear they never knew they had to make a lasting impact on this world. Bryce is a proud husband and father of three beautiful children. Thankfully, his wife, McKenzie, became a lifelong fan after they met in first grade. Bryce's story is one of inspiration and perseverance, proving that anything is possible if you are simply willing to take more risks, have more faith, and be more creative to shift gears along the way.